Agriculture
at the Border

Canada–U.S. Trade Relations
in the Global Food Regime

Agriculture at the Border

Canada–U.S. Trade Relations in the Global Food Regime

edited by Gregory P. Marchildon

CANADIAN PLAINS RESEARCH CENTER
2000

Canadian Plains Research Center
University of Regina
Regina, Saskatchewan S4S 0A2
Canada
Tel: (306) 585-4758
Fax: (306) 585-4699
e-mail: canadian.plains@uregina.ca
http://www.cprc.uregina.ca

Canadian Cataloguing in Publication Data
Main entry under title:
Agriculture at the border
        (Canadian Plains reprint series, ISSN 1208-9680 ; 6)

Reprint of papers published in American review of Canadian studies, v. 28, no. 3. The papers are based on papers presented at the Association for Canadian Studies in the United States Biennial Conference in Minneapolis in 1997.
    Includes bibliographical references and index.
    ISBN 0-88977-140-5

1. Produce industry and trade—Canada. 2. Produce industry and trade—United States. 3. Canada—Commerce—United States. 4. United States—Commerce—Canada. I. Marchildon, Gregory P., 1956–   II. Association for Canadian Studies in the United States. Conference (14th : 1997 : Minneapolis, Minn.).
III. University of Regina. Canadian Plains Research Center.
IV. Title: American review of Canadian studies. V. Series.

HD9014.C32A34 2000   382'.41'0971   C00-920009-6

Cover Design: Donna Achtzehner, Canadian Plains Research Center
Cover Photo by David Jonasson

Printed and bound in Canada by
Houghton-Boston, Saskatoon, Saskatchewan

Printed on acid-free paper

Table of Contents

Introduction

Agriculture at the Border: Canada-U.S. Trade Relations in the Global Food Regime

The essays in this book originated in a group of papers presented on prairie issues at the Association of Canadian Studies in the United States Biennial Conference in Minneapolis in November 1997. These papers were then reworked as published articles for a special theme issue of the Association's quarterly, the *American Review of Canadian Studies*. This was the first time that agriculture and its impact on the relations between Canada and the United States was profiled in this journal to a readership interested in a broad range of scholarship on Canadian subjects as diverse as literature and politics.

By publishing these essays in book form, the Canadian Plains Research Center is reaching beyond "Canadianists" to those whose lives depend upon the agri-food industry in the prairie region of North America. In addition, students and scholars tilling the fields of agricultural economics, international trade policy as well as public policy should find the essays illuminating. Most of the authors are prominent agricultural economists with extensive policy and industry experience on both sides of the border. All were asked to write for a general audience, avoiding the technical terms of their profession in favour of a straightforward and rather simple presentation.

The volume begins with a concise, two-century history of agriculture in the context of the Canadian-American relationship. All six of the subsequent essays focus on the state of contemporary agricultural trade relations. The issues raised by the authors—from disputes over subsidies and dumping to concerns about the policy instruments employed by the respective national governments—have become difficult challenges in the current environment. Presently, farm commodity prices are at an historic low. As a result, net income for Canadian prairie grain farmers is well below the total costs of production when taking into consideration the return to capital, labour, management and land.

In Saskatchewan, for example, 1998 realized net farm income fell 29 percent below the previous (1993-97) five-year average. In July 1999, Agriculture and Agri-food Canada forecast that Saskatchewan realized net farm income would be -$48 million, including payments from the existing safety net of crop insurance, the Net Income

Stabilization Account (NISA) and Agricultural Income Disaster Assistance (AIDA).[1] This has translated into extreme hardship for farmers and those around them, including farm equipment dealers who have seen a 68 percent drop in sales from 1997 to 1999.[2]

There are a number of complex reasons for the current situation but they can be divided into two main categories. On the supply side, larger than average global crop production has served to keep commodity prices down, a problem that has been exacerbated by the ongoing impact of—as well as recent increases in—farm subsidies in the European Union and the United States. And on the demand side, the poor performance of key Pacific Basin economies such as Japan and Taiwan, among others, has translated into less purchasing power for grains and oilseeds from North America. The result has been close to catastrophic for farm commodity prices. Relative to the five-year average of 1994-98, the selling prices of durum wheat and peas have declined by 39 percent, canola by 34 percent, flax by 25 percent, and spring wheat by 24 percent.[3]

In the case of prairie farmers in Canada, the situation has been aggravated by the recent removal of domestic subsidies, including freight rate subsidies under the Western Grain Transportation Act that were eliminated in 1995. In addition, unlike farmers south of the border, Canadian farmers have not received billions of dollars in aid from their central government to cope with the situation. By 1998, European wheat subsidies had reached 56 percent of farm gate value for wheat while American subsidies had grown to 38 percent, far outstripping the 9 percent producer subsidy for Canadian wheat farmers.[4]

This is the difficult environment in which relations between Canada and the United States are now conducted. Farmers on both sides of the border are caught in a cost-price squeeze and are demanding temporary support from their respective governments. Not surprisingly, each blames the other to some extent for their current difficulties. American farmers in the northern tier states target imports of Canadian grain as well as the Canadian Wheat Board as the villains in the piece. Canadian prairie farmers point to American subsidies, which have risen sharply in retaliation to even larger European farm subsidies, as the chief cause of lower market prices.

As the first historical essay points out, this is not the first time that Canada-US relations have been adversely affected by low agricultural commodity prices. The Great Depression was caused, in part, by a precipitous fall in grain commodity prices. With North American farmers cutting their purchases of farm equipment and automobiles, industrial production slowed and industrial stock prices began to plunge. This led directly to a rise in protectionism, first in the United States through the Smoot-Hawley Tariff Act of 1930, and then in Canada through the Ottawa Agreements of 1932. While agriculture makes up a much smaller percentage of our respective national economies today, farming remains a mainstay of the regional prairie economy, and the consequences for this part of the continent could be severe if grain, pulse and oilseed prices remain low for an extended period.

While agricultural trade between Canada and the United States has grown steadily during the 1980s and 1990s, the most remarkable change has been the dramatic growth in Canadian grain, beef and pork exports south of the border since the implementation of the Canada-United States Free Trade Agreement (FTA). The factors that have caused this export boom, and the consequences for producers, distributors, processors and governments on both sides of the border, are the subject of all the essays that follow the historical introduction.

Richard Gray and Mel Annand of the University of Saskatchewan examine the economic and legal environment that has fuelled recent dramatic increases in Canadian grain (wheat, barley, flax, canola, oats and rye) exports to the United States. In the authors' words, answering the question of why this has occurred is necessary, given that grain exports to one of the world's largest producers of such crops is a little like "carrying coals to Newcastle." Gray and Annand put forward a number of reasons for this trend. They include the legal changes wrought by the FTA (and as carried forward through NAFTA), the economic impact of the American Export Enhancement Program (EEP), and the removal of Canadian transportation subsidies.

Demcey Johnson of North Dakota State University also puts great emphasis on the impact of the removal of Canadian rail transportation subsidies in 1995. As the cost of shipping grain to port increased substantially, Canadian grain exporters began to look south of the border for less distant customers. With Canadian grain plugging up grain-handling distribution at some border points, American farmers were angered by reduced access to their own system, and this led directly to the (mistaken) perception that the Canadians were not playing by the rules. While rejecting some of the allegations, including dumping and taking advantage of a lower Canadian dollar, Johnson focuses on the impact of the Canadian system of grain quality controls and the Canadian Wheat Board. The latter institution in particular, along with the regulatory and policy environment supporting it, is now drawing the hostile attention of American producers and politicians in their efforts to resolve what they call the "Canadian grain problem." Indeed, the US government has made it clear that it intends to try and change the provisions surrounding state trading enterprises in the current round of World Trade Organization (WTO) negotiations.

Hartley Furtan and Kathy Baylis of the Universities of Saskatchewan and Laval focus on the Canadian Wheat Board in their analysis of the prevalence of state trading in wheat throughout the world. They describe the characteristics that have been used by the WTO and its GATT predecessor to define a state trading enterprise (STE). They then explore the extent to which the Canadian Wheat Board does and does not constitute an STE. They also describe in detail the fundamentally different perceptions of the Canadian Wheat Board on both sides of the border. In their essay, William Wilson and Bruce Dahl of North Dakota State University point to the Canadian Wheat Board as one of the major policy and institutional differences between Canada and the United States.

Nonetheless, as pointed out by Wilson and Dahl, the outstanding fact is the degree to which both countries have commercially integrated since the early 1990s, again partly due to the impact of the free trade agreements. Before this time, Cargill was the only major American grain-handling firm operating in a Canadian market dominated by a handful of private Canadian companies and cooperatives such as the Saskatchewan Wheat Pool. Since then, ConAgra has constructed grain terminals throughout the Canadian Prairies and Archer Daniels Midland (ADM) and General Mills have moved in through strategic alliances with existing Canadian firms. Meanwhile, separate Canadian and American flour milling and malting firms have merged into North American companies.

Policy integration is the subject of the essay by Larry Martin, Vincent Amanor-Boadu and Fiona Stirling of the University of Guelph. They examine the similarities and differences in Canadian and American trade remedy laws, concluding that while some "harmonization" has occurred since the 1980s, important differences remain. They then provide a useful and comprehensive summary of the differences in both laws and practice at the end of their essay.

Commercial and policy integration is not restricted to the grains sector. Linda Young and John Marsh of Montana State University demonstrate the extent to which the live cattle markets of the United States and Canada have integrated since the mid-1980s. Again, as in the case of the grain trade, the United States is a much more important market for Canadians than vice versa, with well over one half of all Canadian beef exports flowing to the United States. This is a consequence of tariffs and quotas being reduced and eliminated through the trade agreements as well as sanitary restrictions being reduced. Grading remains one of the challenges to further policy integration but it is evident that previously separate national markets are more accurately described as a single continental market.

In conclusion, prairie producers on both sides of the border are now facing the reality posed by the commercial integration of previously separate agricultural economies. Politicians and policy-makers in both countries face a huge challenge where policy and institutional differences remain. These differences range from trade remedy laws to farm income support mechanisms, and from unique institutions including the Canadian Wheat Board in Canada to the Commercial Credit Corporation in the United States. Low agricultural commodity prices may magnify these differences but it is hoped that the essays that follow throw some light on what will continue to be a heated debate in the years to come.

Gregory P. Marchildon
Regina
December, 1999

NOTES

1. Agriculture and Agri-Food Canada, Data Book, July 1999 update, electronic publication: http://www.agr.ca/policy/epad/english/pubs/dbook/1999/july1999/section.pdf
2. Canadian Farm and Industrial Equipment Institute, Outlook 1999, January 1999, 7.
3. Saskatchewan Agriculture and Food Backgrounder, Presented to the House of Commons Standing Committee on Agriculture, October 28, 1999, 3.
4. Organization for Economic Co-operation and Development, *Agricultural Policies in OECD Countries: Monitoring and Evaluation*, 1999 (Paris: OECD, 1999), 201, 209, 253.

Canadian-American Agricultural Trade Relations: A Brief History

GREGORY P. MARCHILDON

Introduction

Although in recent years some specialized work has been done on the agricultural trade relationship between Canada and the United States, relatively little historical work has been devoted to this subject. This is true despite a voluminous literature—most of which, admittedly, has been written from a Canadian point of view—on the history of Canadian-American relations generally. But, here again, the subject of agricultural trade rarely appears, and then usually only to illustrate a more general problem or conflict. There are a number of likely reasons for this, most prominently the fact that agricultural trade has been on a long-term decline relative to other forms of commodity trade within the world's largest bilateral trading and investment relationship; that is, Canada-U.S. trade has been dominated by manufactured goods for most of the postwar era, leaving agriculture a negligible position. Nonetheless, understanding the history of Canadian-American agricultural trade relations remains important for a number of reasons. First, economic disputes between the two countries have shaped the very nature of the bilateral relationship and, until the 1960s, agricultural trade, along with the fisheries, consistently took top prize as the subject matter of these disputes. Since the early 1960s, disputes over automobiles (rules of origin), culture (Canadian content regulations), and softwood lumber have joined, but not supplanted, these sectoral problem areas, as the recent disputes over salmon and wheat testify.

Second, as Table 1 illustrates, bilateral agricultural exports have been more important than the percentage of total trade between the two countries would appear to indicate. An $18 billion annual trade in agricultural commodities (1996) is sizeable by almost any absolute measure, and the historical importance of this trade was proportionately much greater. During the postwar era, the United States has become Canada's main agricultural trading partner, in both exports and imports, while Canada has remained one of the United States' main partners—since the 1970s, the second largest exporter (after the European Community) to the U.S., and among the top four importers of American agricultural goods. Moreover, because of the very regional nature of this trade, it has had, and continues to have, a disproportionate impact on the lives of Canadians and Americans in regions of both countries including the fruit and vegetable growers of California, the cattle ranchers of Alberta, and the durum wheat growers of Saskatchewan, to cite only a few examples (Cohn 1990, 13-14).

Table 1: Agricultural Exports as a Percentage of Total Bilateral Trade in the United States and Canada, 1992-1996 (millions of dollars)

CANADA	1992	1993	1994	1995	1996
1. Agricultural Exports to the U.S. *	6,942	7,367	8,104	8,590	10,257
2. Total Exports to the U.S.	123,377	149,006	180,837	205,853	221,858
3. % of Ag. Exports to Total Exports	5.63%	4.94%	4.48%	4.17%	4.62%
4. Agricultural Exports to the World	30,679	32,789	37,749	41,968	48,873
5. Total Exports to the World	163,467	190,383	227,892	264,937	280,566
6. % of Ag. Exports to Total Exports	18.77%	17.22%	16.56%	15.84%	17.42%
UNITED STATES					
7. Agricultural Exports to Canada **	5,980	6,417	7,155	7,525	7,925
8. Total Exports to Canada	110,379	130,714	156,342	173,726	181,893
9. % of Ag. Exports to Total Exports	5.42%	4.91%	4.58%	4.33%	4.36%
10. Agricultural Exports to the World	42,238	41,938	44,936	54,850	57,970
11. Total Exports to the World	448,164	465,091	512,626	584,742	623,660
12. % of Ag. Exports to Total Exports	9.42%	9.02%	8.77%	9.38%	9.30%

*   Canadian Agricultural Exports to the U.S. include: grains and oilseeds, livestock, dairy products, eggs, and processed foods.

**   U.S. Agricultural Exports to Canada include: specialty crops, fruits, livestock, dairy products, wool, and cotton.

Note: Line Items 1 through 9 above are calculated in Canada dollars. Line Items 10 through 12 are calculated in U.S. dollars.

SOURCES:
For Line Items 1-9:
        "Canadian Agri-Food Exports to the U.S. by Product Category." *Statistics Canada.* TIERS database, 1996.
        "Canada's Two-way Agri-Food Trade." *Statistics Canada.* TIERS database, 1996.
        "Canadian Statistics—Exports of Goods on a Balance-of-Payments Basis." *Statistics Canada.* CANSIM, Matrix 3685.

For Line Items 10-12:
        "Agricultural Exports: Value by Principal Commodities and Selected Countries." *Statistical Abstract of the U.S.* U.S. Bureau of the Census, 1996. 673 and 805.

The bilateral relationship is shaped by much more than crossborder trade, however. Both countries produce sizeable agricultural surpluses and are, therefore, major competitors for third markets. Indeed, both countries have been major food exporters since the mid-nineteenth century, and agricultural exports to third countries have historically constituted a relatively large share of both countries' exports. During the period 1992-96, for example, approximately 17 percent of total Canadian exports, and roughly 9 percent of total American exports, were agricultural in origin, whereas only 5 percent of total bilateral trade involved agricultural products (see Table 1). And while both countries individually have been major exporters, together they constitute the most powerful exporting bloc within the global food regime. This is a consequence of a number of factors, including the amount of land available for agricultural purposes as well as being at the forefront of the mechanization and commercialization of agriculture in the nineteenth century, including the assembling, handling, financing, and transporting of agricultural commodities for export.

Of course, unlike the member countries of the European Union, the two countries have rarely acted as a bloc and the United States has been, and remains, the more important of the two because of its larger agricultural land base and its more varied climatic and soil conditions, which permit a broader range of food production. However, with a much smaller domestic population, Canada has consistently exported a much larger percentage of its agricultural output than the United States has, and Canada's producers have traditionally been much more dependent on foreign markets.

The following brief history of the bilateral relationship has been divided up into eras, each with its own relatively unique set of characteristics. By use of this periodization and characterization, I hope to capture the main trends in the relationship as well as the global changes that have helped to shape bilateral relations.

Early Bilateral Relations, 1800-1866

These early decades witnessed a settlement, investment, and transportation pattern that would form the foundation for commercialized agriculture in North America. The bilateral relationship was characterized by an openness between the two economies and, in some instances, a surprising degree of integration in certain agricultural markets. British mercantilist armor in the form of the Corn Laws and the Navigation Acts was intended to keep British North America as British and un-American as possible. To some extent these laws fulfilled their purpose in giving colonists privileged access to a vast and growing market for foodstuffs. However, these laws could not prevent a crossborder convenience trade in agricultural commodities, and settlers on both sides of the border regularly sold grain, livestock, and animals for breeding, often avoiding tariffs by using unmonitored sections of the border.

When the United States imposed a tariff of twenty-five cents per bushel on wheat in 1824, however, this cut severely into the convenience trade in grain that had been steadily building up between the two countries. The loss of this market was offset the following year when Britain permitted colonial wheat and flour to be admitted at all times into the British market, not just when the country was suffering severe shortages as had previously been the general rule. In 1828, after lobbying by Canadian merchants who were trying to spur the local grain-milling industry and make Montreal the principal North American port for wheat exports (in competition with an alternate route to New York provided by the newly built Erie Canal), the British government agreed to allow flour ground in Canada from American grain to be admitted into the British market as any other colonial grain or flour. This encouraged a reverse flow of grain north as American producers took advantage of this loophole by shipping their grain north to Canadian millers (Fornari 1976, 138; Marr and Paterson 1980, 93, 98, 124-34).

When Britain formally adopted free trade by eliminating the Corn Laws in 1846, the Montreal merchants were left in shock, having become dependent on this artificial trade flow. Their vision of an empire of the St. Lawrence in tatters, many of these same merchants began to promote annexation to the United States as the only solution to their business problems. Others pushed for a moderate solution—a reciprocity agreement between the two countries that would allow natural (unprocessed or semi-processed) goods like agricultural commodities to cross the border without duties, thereby restoring the convenience trade between the two countries and allowing for large-scale exports from British North America to the United States whenever crops failed or fell short south of the border.

To restore economic stability without allowing its colonies to fall into the political grasp of the United States, the British government supported the Reciprocity Agreement of 1854. The agreement would last until 1866, when it was abrogated by the United States largely in an effort to strike back at Great Britain for its tacit support of the South during the Civil War. During these years, crossborder trade grew dramatically, with agricultural and forest products constituting 85 percent of British North American exports to the United States (Officer and Smith 1968). As can be seen in Table 2, bilateral agricultural trade soared to new heights, continuing to grow even after the termination of the Reciprocity Agreement. By the outbreak of the Civil War, this trade in wheat, barley, oats, flour, livestock, meat, and dairy products had become more than a convenience trade. In addition, the agreement created, at least for a time, a relatively integrated North American transportation system in which wheat harvested in Illinois could be shipped to Britain or Europe from Montreal via the Great Lakes and St. Lawrence system, or grain grown in Upper Canada could be shipped from New York via Buffalo and the Erie Canal. Whatever the actual impact of the agreement, it was identified with prosperity by many Canadians, particularly farmers, perpetuating requests for free trade with the United States for generations to come.

The Post-Civil War and Post-Confederation Booms, 1867-1913

After the Civil War, the era was characterized by rapid westward expansion of commercialized agriculture in both countries, world leadership in the logistics of handling and transporting food products, an intense rivalry for the rapidly expanding British market, and a bilateral relationship marked by high protection. All of this took place against a backdrop of increasing international specialization of production with Britain, then the world's most industrial nation, fast becoming the world's major food importer, and with Canada and the United States becoming the leading food exporters in the world. At the same time, the end of the Civil War marked the beginning of the final push west, with Americans joined by immigrants settling in the new agricultural lands of Kansas, Nebraska, Minnesota, and the Dakotas. Canadians and recent immigrants to Canada joined this flow to the American West by the hundreds of thousands.[1] This emigration from Canada would not be reversed until the turn of the century when settlers, including hundreds of thousands of Americans, began to pour into the "last best West," with Saskatchewan and Alberta "by far the preferred destinations" (Widdis 1997, 241).[2]

During these years, most settlers traveled to their new homesteads on trains that crisscrossed the North American continent. These same trains would serve to move their agricultural commodities to both domestic

Table 2: Canadian-American Agricultural Trade, 1850-1870
(millions of dollars)

	Canadian Exports to the United States		American Exports to Canada	
Year	Grains & Flour	Animals &Products	Grain & Flour	Animals &Products
1850	2.21	0.107	0.19	0.013
1851	1.72	0.124	0.34	0.016
1852	1.65	0.127	0.36	0.013
1853	1.95	0.108	0.21	0.022
1854	3.89	0.136	0.62	0.034
total	11.42 avg. 2.28	0.602 avg. 0.12	1.72 avg. 0.34	0.098 avg. 0.02
1855	8.17	1.522	0.85	0.128
1856	10.83	1.792	2.71	0.198
1857	10.53	2.099	2.58	0.191
1858	5.29	1.489	3.76	0.097
1859	5.82	1.867	2.84	0.133
total	40.64 avg. 8.12	8.769 avg. 1.75	12.74 avg. 2.59	0.747 avg. 0.15
1860	8.97	2.368	2.26	0.112
1861	9.38	2.394	4.31	0.246
1862	7.74	2.222	4.33	0.278
1863	5.74	2.229	7.82	0.391
1864	10.71	4.881	6.31	0
total	42.54 avg. 8.81	14.09 avg. 2.82	25.03 avg. 5.11	1.027 avg. 0.21
1865	10.74	6.85	6.92	0.354
1866	13.83	10.24	2.86	0.227
1867	7.25	2.18	1.71	0.076
1868	0	0	6.05	0.001
1869	6.88	5.61	3.79	0
1870	6.64	10.57	9.31	0
total	45.34 avg. 9.06	35.45 avg. 5.91	30.64 avg. 5.39	0.658 avg. 0.11
total	139.93	58.92	70.12	2.53

Notes: Canadian Exports include: wheat, barley, oats, flour, livestock, meat, and wool.
American Exports include: wheat, flour, butter, and cheese.
Based on U.S. returns only, except for butter and cheese which is based on
Canadian returns.

Source: Calculated from L.H. Officer and L.B. Smith, "The Canadian-American Reciprocity Treaty of 1855 to 1866." *Journal of Economic History* 28(1968): 616.

and foreign markets using cars specially built to carry grains, livestock, and refrigerated meats. Supplemented by shipping through the Great Lakes and canals, this transportation network would emerge as one of the largest and most efficient in the world. This period also saw both countries become world leaders in the assembling, handling, and financing of agricultural commodities transported over long distances to market within North America and exported, mainly to Europe. The elevator system in particular, with its large-scale storage and bulk handling, inspection, and grade standardization attracted foreign attention and imitation. Financial instruments and organizations were created to facilitate large-scale exports over long distances, including futures contracts and the commodity exchanges in which they were traded. Most of these innovations first appeared in the United States but were rapidly adopted and, in the case of inspections and grade standardization, improved upon in Canada by the early 1900s (Fornari 1976, 142; Rothstein 1960, 418).

By the time that new western settlement had slowed, the United States had more land available for agricultural purposes than virtually any other country in the world, with Canada falling in about the sixth rank behind other enormous countries such as Russia and China. This gave both countries a comparative advantage in agriculture relative to more densely populated and comparatively small western-European countries, particularly Britain, which had the largest urban industrial work force in the world at the beginning of this era. Exports of wheat, as well as meat and dairy products, to Britain climbed steadily from 1867 until the beginning of the Great War, with both countries competing vigorously for an ever-larger share of the British market. During these years, too, Britain purchased at least 50 percent of the wheat and flour exported from the United States, and an even larger percentage of Canada's wheat exports. In absolute terms, however, Canada was not really even in the running until wheat exports from its new western frontier came on stream during the first decade of the twentieth century. As can be seen in Table 3, Canadian exports did not exceed American exports until 1910, and then only temporarily. Not until the interwar years would Canadian wheat and flour exports regularly outstrip American exports to Britain (Rothstein 1960).

While exports to the rest of the world were growing rapidly, crossborder trade in agricultural commodities was being artificially dampened by high tariffs—particularly on the American side. What were planned as temporary tariffs used to raise money during the Civil War were retained after it ended and, with the abrogation of the Reciprocity

Table 3: British Grain and Flour Imports from the United States
and Canada, 1874-1934 (cwts.)*

Year	U.K. Imports from Canada	U.K. Imports from U.S.	Year	U.K. Imports from Canada	U.K. Imports from U.S.
1874	4,298,315	27,206,052	1904	9,036,643	19,152,547
1875	4,069,565	26,372,200	1905	8,369,391	14,831,164
1876	2,776,975	22,223,403	1906	13,283,700	36,655,469
1877	3,265,174	23,594,005	1907	15,207,194	33,462,842
1878	2,999,400	33,588,160	1908	17,920,476	39,600,621
total	17,409,429	132,983,820	total	63,817,404	143,702,643
1879	5,353,697	44,619,619	1909	19,476,023	25,127,726
1880	4,543,407	44,783,100	1910	20,315,451	18,065,261
1881	3,200,434	45,699,956	1911	18,913,656	20,045,355
1882	3,115,769	44,888,181	1912	27,112,040	25,824,833
1883	2,428,417	40,216,835	1913	27,577,571	42,620,227
total	18,641,724	220,207,691	total	113,394,741	131,683,402
1884	2,651,954	36,065,051	1918	23,697,450	49,706,360
1885	2,113,797	39,709,567	1919	25,595,594	46,038,842
1886	4,108,186	39,882,249	1920	13,409,679	53,529,800
1887	5,262,791	50,611,905	1921	22,736,459	47,038,255
1888	2,165,042	31,847,188	1922	32,071,522	43,618,429
total	16,301,770	198,115,960	total	117,510,704	239,931,686
1889	2,793,383	30,958,647	1923	36,237,495	36,793,294
1890	2,424,768	33,903,560	1924	46,055,032	35,331,617
1891	4,603,349	43,226,948	1925	35,527,385	30,343,100
1892	5,763,677	60,924,785	1926	43,148,149	34,978,414
1893	4,658,724	57,256,738	1927	39,305,087	39,668,620
total	20,243,901	226,270,678	1928	47,782,628	26,320,384
1894	4,488,822	46,787,976	total	248,055,776	203,435,429
1895	5,099,183	45,322,801	1929	32,363,027	25,788,800
1896	6,302,233	52,785,317	1930	32,412,417	25,446,510
1897	6,946,458	54,135,102	1931	32,506,740	14,127,203
1898	7,746,474	62,085,605	1932	52,372,968	5,277,234
total	30,583,170	261,116,801	1933	51,574,697	170,165
1899	8,727,236	60,214,254	1934	41,573,009	310,094
1900	7,997,626	57,418,064	total	242,802,858	71,120,006
1901	8,577,960	66,855,025	TOTAL	940,756,273	2,124,747,930
1902	12,226,490	64,961,474			
1903	14,465,484	46,730,727	*cwts = 1 hundredweight = 112 pounds		
total	51,994,796	296,179,544	= 50.8 kilograms		

Source: *Statistical Abstract for the United Kingdom*, Her Majesty's Stationery Office, London.
No. 31(1869-83): 60-61; No. 40(1878-92):78-79; No. 53(1891-1905): 134-135; No. 61(1899-1913):
176-177; No. 76(1913 and 1918-31): 360; No. 79(1913 and 1921-34): 271.

Agreement in 1866, natural goods from Canada including agricultural commodities were no longer exempt from these high duties. Tariffs, moreover, continued to climb until 1913. One exception to this was the lowering of the barley tariff in 1883 at the insistence of the American breweries; they demanded access to high-quality Canadian malting barley. When even this tariff was raised from 10 cents to 30 cents a bushel by the 1890 McKinley Tariff in order to protect northern American barley farmers, it wiped out what had quickly become a substantial crossborder barley trade (Taussig 1967, 248-9, 274-5; Hart 1996, 3). When it became obvious to Canadians that a new reciprocity deal with the United States for agricultural commodities, forest products, and other natural goods was impossible politically, they concluded that they might strengthen the country's future bargaining position by imposing higher protectionist tariffs of their own in 1879. The immediate result, however, was to curb even further the potential for a vigorous crossborder trade.

When Wilfrid Laurier first became Prime Minister in 1896, any notion of free trade in nonmanufactured goods with the United States seemed highly unlikely but, by 1910, an unanticipated window of opportunity suddenly opened. Free-trade agitation by farmers and populists on both sides of the border had grown to the point that both governments felt the need to let off some of the pressure by negotiating a new reciprocity agreement that would lower or eliminate tariffs on all natural goods, including most agricultural commodities. In Canada, the deal was made contingent on the outcome of the 1911 election—one which Laurier lost, disappointing populists, free traders, and many farmers north and south of the border. Although the wall between the two countries was very briefly lowered with the U.S. Tariff Act of 1913—when duties on wheat, flour, livestock, meats, eggs, and dairy products were reduced—the dislocation about to be caused by a world war would soon push the United States back onto a more protectionist track.

War, Dislocation, and Protectionism, 1914-1939

One of the overriding characteristics of this era was a breakdown of the pre-1914 global trading system and the move to greater protectionism. Rejecting the experiment with freer trade begun in 1913, the United States returned to a policy of higher tariffs in 1921, while Canada began increasing its tariffs in 1930. By 1933, both countries reached a protectionist high-water mark. Although the disruption caused by the Great War would stimulate a temporary increase in the demand for foodstuffs from North America—wheat and meat in particular—demand would decline by the late 1920s, leading to low prices and decreasing exports to third countries. This, together with drought and crop failures would, by the early 1930s, lead to an absolute decline in world exports as well as a precipitous decline in bilateral trade. As a result, farm cash income fell by 67 percent in Canada and 62 percent in the United States in 1930-34 relative to the period 1925-29, a statistic that translated into extreme hardship for farmers on both sides of the border (Hamilton and Drummond 1959, 41).

World War One provided the United States with more effective protection for its manufactured goods from European competition than any tariff. The war's end was followed by a recession in 1921, leading to a sharp fall in the world price of grain; this put an end to the low-tariff policy (Fornari 1976, 144-6). That same year, President Harding pushed through the Emergency Tariff Act and, in 1923, the highly protective Fordney-McCumber tariff was passed. These acts set the tone for the next two decades. Although aimed directly at preventing European manufactured goods from entering the United States, the duties on agricultural commodities—which had been exported from Canada free of any duties since 1913—were raised. Wheat now had a duty of thirty cents per bushel, rye fifteen cents a bushel, beef three cents a pound, and so on. Then, in 1924, after an investigation of production cost differentials between the two countries for hard winter wheat by the U.S. Tariff Commission, the tariff on wheat was raised to forty-two cents per bushel (Taussig 1967, 455-6).

Given the already high tariffs, Canadians were shocked when Republican presidential nominee Herbert Hoover advocated even higher duties on agricultural imports to aid the American farmer in 1928. Crossborder agricultural trade, already hit hard by earlier tariff increases, was now being threatened with extinction, and Hoover's election would soon prompt retaliation on the other side of the border, starting an agricultural tariff war. For its part, William Lyon Mackenzie King's Liberal government had initially thought that relatively low tariffs, particularly on nonmanufactured goods, might dissuade Congress from implementing Hoover's election promise. But when the Senate raised the duties on a number of agricultural products in March of 1930, the Canadian government targeted key American imports, including fruits and vegetables, as well as food exports that competed with American exports in the global marketplace. The higher duties in the Canadian budget that May were accompanied by a "countervail" clause aimed squarely at the United States, warning that any future duties which exceeded the levels in the Canadian schedule would be met by similar increases by the Canadian government. King hoped that his saber rattling would be enough to prevent Hoover from fully implementing his earlier election promises but Hoover, encouraged by what was turning out to be an almost 40 percent drop in American farm commodity prices that year alone, signed the Smoot-Hawley Tariff Act into law on 17 June 1930 (Fausold 1990, 372). This was unfortunate timing for King, who had just called an election, and his opponent, Conservative R.B. Bennett, advocated even more vigorous retaliation against the United States. The tariff on agricultural goods became the major, if not the dominating, issue of the campaign, and helped defeat Mackenzie King on 28 July 1930 (Kottman 1975).

Canadian exports to the United States were gradually choked off by the tariff increases from 1921 until the knock-out punch delivered by the Smoot-Hawley Tariff of 1930. Wheat exports, which were worth $102 million in 1920-21 dropped to $6.6 million by 1930-31, while livestock and wool exports had fallen to less than $1 million by the 1930-31 season. Beginning in 1930, the Canadian response was more of the same—to choke off American exports to Canada with annual increases in the tariff, culminating in an unprecedented 30 percent hike in 1933 (Taussig 1967, 504-5; Granatstein 1985, 30). In addition, R. B. Bennett used Canada's position in the British Empire to retaliate against the United States. At the 1932 Ottawa Conference of empire countries, he convinced the United Kingdom to impose new or higher duties on wheat and dairy products from outside the empire, allowing countries such as Canada, Australia, and New Zealand to displace American agricultural exports to the U.K.[3] The Ottawa agreements of 1932 played an important role in reducing the American share of total British imports (the majority of which were agricultural products) from 16.5 percent in 1929 to 11.1 percent in 1936. In the specific case of grain and flour, the American share of the British market dropped like a stone; Canadian exports filled the gap, as Table 3 illustrates. Indeed, by 1932, British imports of Canadian wheat and flour were more than ten times greater than equivalent imports from the United States. The same kind of trade diversion occurred in other commodities and, by 1936, the U.K. was taking 62 percent of Canadian farm goods as compared to only 21 percent of American agricultural commodities (Drummond and Hillmer 1989, 12-23).

Cordell Hull, President Roosevelt's secretary of state, claimed that 40 percent of American trade with Britain had been destroyed by the new imperial preferences, and used the Reciprocal Trade Agreements Act of 1934 to fight against the Ottawa agreements. The result was a series of agreements with countries that created holes in imperial preferences. The 1935 agreement struck between the United States, Britain, and Canada, followed by a Canadian-American accord in 1938, mitigated the impact of the Ottawa agreements, at least for semi-processed and manufactured products. It is questionable, however, whether the 1935 and 1938 agreements had much of an impact on bilateral trade in grain and livestock, given the exemption written into the agreement by the United States to protect the operation of its domestic agricultural policies (Hart 1996, 4). These New Deal policies included production controls and price supports, food distribution and export subsidies, farm credit subsidies, as well as crop insurance and disaster payments. Central to this dense network of subsides and supports was the Agricultural Adjustment Act (AAA) (Pasour 1990, 74).

The two main provisions of the AAA were section 22, which provided domestic price maintenance, and section 32, which authorized the use of tariff revenues to subsidize agricultural exports. The Commodity Credit Corporation (CCC) was established at the same time. The CCC paid farmers by setting the "loan rates"—the amount that the government was willing to pay for basic agricultural commodities such as wheat and cotton. Droughts in 1934 and 1936 eliminated the surplus of such commodities for most of the 1930s but the loan rate was set above the world rate for the first time in 1938-39. Ordinarily this would have served to reduce wheat exports to Europe but those markets were closing because of the outbreak of the war and the impact of the loan rate was limited to Canada. At first, the spread between the subsidized American prices and the Canadian price was attractive enough to encourage Americans to import Canadian wheat or flour despite the tariff of forty-two cents a bushel. As a consequence, the United States used the authority of the AAA to impose import quotas to prevent Canadian wheat and flour from flowing south (Evans 1971, 66-8). The use of this legislation would become even more extensive during and after World War Two.

The Canadian agricultural policy response to the Great Depression was weak in comparison to the New Deal initiatives south of the border. In 1935, the Canadian Wheat Board (CWB) was set up to help market wheat on behalf of Canadian producers in the face of chronically low world demand. First used to manage Canadian wheat exports when World War

One disrupted markets, the CWB had been quickly dismantled. When reestablished in 1935, it was not given a monopoly over sales, and the board's power and impact were consequently quite limited. Not even the broad panoply of American policies, however, was as effective as the Second World War in delivering the demand and price conditions required for prosperity.

Prosperity and Security in Agricultural Trade Relations, 1940-1985

The decades that followed the Great Depression were relatively prosperous ones for North American agriculture. This new era was marked by a substantial increase in bilateral trade and greater harmony in Canadian-American agricultural trade relations. Trying to regenerate a world market for their products and services, both countries worked together to construct a more liberalized trade order through the ITO/GATT negotiations. However, this understanding did not extend to agriculture because of the political need in the United States to protect the agricultural support system that had been established during the New Deal. The era also witnessed the decline of Britain as the world's largest food importer, the rise of Europe as a major agricultural exporter, and the proliferation of important new markets in the Soviet Union, China, and the Pacific basin generally.

World War Two turned agricultural surpluses into shortages and low prices into rising prices, which benefited farmers on both sides of the border. Those hardest hit by the Great Depression, cash crop farmers such as wheat farmers, recovered the fastest. At the same time, war meant that agriculture would be harnessed to both countries' war efforts. The Canadian Wheat Board was given monopoly powers in 1943 and was merely one part of the extensive machinery put in place by Canada in order to control production, prices, and exports of basic commodities, including foodstuffs, for the purposes of the war effort. The United States also beefed up its price supports and controls. In 1941, Congress extended price support to nonbasic agricultural goods, including dairy products, by amending the Commodity Credit Corporation Appropriation Act, and then raised these mandatory price supports to 92.5 percent in 1942. In 1944, the CCC's borrowing power was increased and it was authorized to sell from its stocks for export at below domestic prices (Evans 1971, 70). It was this extension of the control and power of these New Deal institutions, and their popularity among producers as well as the companies that assembled, transported, and exported basic agricultural commodities, which led to Congress and the Executive taking a defensive position during the ITO/ GATT negotiations immediately after the war. Paradoxically, this position would produce both a common agenda and conflict with Canada.

On the one hand, producers in both countries benefited from the various subsidy, support, and stabilization programs which marked both postwar economies. Their experience with planning during the war stood in stark contrast to the breakdown of the global market during the interwar years. As a result, few American or Canadian politicians advocated a return to unfettered markets in the case of agriculture. The trend went in the opposite direction. The United States expanded its plethora of New Deal policies and, by the 1970s, Canada had introduced an extensive system of supply management in the egg, dairy, and poultry industries, as well as safety nets for grain producers. On the other hand, the Canadian capacity for certain types of support was constrained by a small population and thus a small tax base. Export subsidies for grain, for example, were difficult to afford relative to the United States, given the much larger percentage of grain that was earmarked for export. This difference resulted in a conflict between the two countries during the immediate postwar ITO/GATT negotiations.

Congressional approval of the International Trade Organization depended on ensuring that any agreement on trade would not endanger the production and export subsidies as well as import quotas that were central to the operation of the Agricultural Adjustment Act and the Commodity Credit Corporation. As a consequence, the American delegation at the ITO/GATT negotiations sought an exemption that would permit member countries to restrict agricultural imports in order to enforce domestic support mechanisms dependent on domestic production limitations. This exception, which became Article XI of the General Agreement on Tariffs and Trade (GATT) was called the "United States Exception" because it was so clearly aimed at meeting American concerns (Evans 1971, 70-1). Knowing that the American negotiators needed flexibility, the Canadian delegation was prepared to live with a partial exemption. Indeed the draft language used came directly out of the 1935 and 1938 reciprocal trade agreements with Canada in which the United States sought a similar exception, but Canadian negotiators nonetheless fought hard against allowing a blanket exception for export subsidies. The Canadians put forward draft language that would at least have limited the use of agricultural export subsidies, but the American negotiators stuck to their guns in order to preserve flexibility in the use of their domestic policy instrument (Hart 1996, 12).

Wheat remained the most important export commodity from North America in the postwar era, and both countries tried to impose some stability over a volatile world market by negotiating wheat agreements. Assuming that Britain would quickly reestablish itself as the largest importer of Canadian food products immediately following the war, and to obtain the security that this market afforded, the Canadian government entered into a long-term agreement for the purchase of Canadian wheat by Britain at below world market prices in 1946. The agreement disappointed Canadian farmers as world prices soon rose far above the contractual amount. Even as a loss leader for future British purchases, however, the Canadian-British Wheat Agreement of 1946 did not prove to be the foundation for a much larger agricultural trading relationship. The truth was that Britain was no longer a wealthy country and no longer at the very center of the global food system as she had been for almost a century (Bothwell and English 1977).

Security for Canadian food exports would now have to be sought through larger arrangements such as the International Wheat Agreement of 1949, in which five of the major world producers—the United States, Canada, Australia, France, and Uruguay, with the Soviet Union and Argentina remaining out—agreed to sell 456 million bushels of wheat annually for five years within an agreed-upon maximum and minimum range of prices, which was set at $1.50 to $1.80 per bushel in 1949-50 down to $1.20 to $1.80 by 1952-53. The Canadian quota of 203 million bushels, combined with the American share of 168 million bushels amounted to 81 percent of the total quota, demonstrating the extent to which North America dominated world wheat exports in the early postwar era. Ten importers guaranteed purchases of various volumes within the price band, the United Kingdom being the largest, guaranteeing a minimum purchase of 177 million bushels, followed by Italy (forty million), India (thirty-eight million), Holland (twenty million), Belgium (twenty million), and various other countries at under one million bushels each (MacGibbon 1952, 144-52). Nothing so elaborate was signed after the expiration of the 1949 agreement, in part because the ultimate trade-off between security and profit turned out to be tipped too far in favor of security in the eyes of the exporting countries, particularly as the world price of wheat continued to improve.

The most significant change in the postwar world was the shift in the role of Western Europe from the world's major food importer to one of its largest exporters. With the creation of the Common Market came two major changes that lie at the heart of this shift. First, as the less-endowed and less-efficient farmers within the member countries faced the brunt of new competition from within the community, they demanded support from it. Second, relatively low-cost agricultural producers—Italian fruit and vegetable growers and French wheat producers—naturally wanted the European market to themselves and demanded greater protection against agricultural imports from outside the community, including from Canada and the United States. The compromise between these two sets of interests was enshrined in the Common Agricultural Policy (CAP), in which basic commodities including grains, vegetables, wine, meat, and dairy products were exempted from the general rules of competition that applied to most other commodities within the Common Market. As Evans points out, CAP provided a very general framework for the "compulsory coordination of national market organizations," and left the details to be worked out by the European Commission (1971, 82-5). The system that emerged by the early 1960s was a comprehensive and rich system of producer supports and subsidies protected by import restrictions and export subsidies. Although the means differed substantially from the American and Canadian systems of supports, subsidies, and stabilization, the intended effect was the same. Moreover, the Europeans used the exemption provided by Article XI of the GATT to defend their exports against possible trade actions by the North Americans.

Under this system, European agricultural production grew dramatically, with surpluses being exported throughout the world. As a consequence, not only were Canadian and American agricultural exports at a disadvantage in the European market but both countries faced increased competition in other third markets. Both countries saw their percentage share of wheat export sales fall from a combined value of 68.3 percent share of world exports in 1950-59 to 57.9 percent share in 1980-89. Over the same period, however, the countries forming the current European Union went from being net importers (with the exception of France which had always been an exporter) to net exporters holding a 16.2 percent share of the world market by 1980-89.

Conclusion

This brief survey has sought to illuminate the main themes in Canada-U.S. agricultural trade relations over two centuries. While the history of this bilateral trading relationship can be broken into several distinct periods, each with its own unique set of characteristics, three consistent themes are discernible. First, from an historical perspective, it is clear that domestic political protection of agricultural export producers has consistently disrupted and impeded what would otherwise have been natural trade flows between Canada and the United States. The political need to protect domestic interests has consistently outweighed the economic rationale governing the bilateral trading relationship. For example, the American retreat into protectionism and isolationism during the interwar years can be attributed in part to the dominant interests of American farmers. Similarly, domestic agricultural interests prevented the United States from adhering to a logically coherent position in the establishment of the global trading order following the Second World War. In Canada, the fear of the abrogation the Canada-U.S. Reciprocity Agreement of 1854 and the resulting loss of a major market for Canadian agricultural products helped push the British North American colonies into political union, and the inability to restore this agreement led directly to the Macdonald government's high tariff National Policy of 1878-79.

Second, the ongoing trade rivalry between the two nations for third markets has led to significant political tension. By the middle of the 1980s this competition had become so fierce that the U.S. government felt compelled to introduce the Export Enhancement Program (EEP). Since that time, the Canadian Wheat Board has been increasingly accused of nontransparency and subsidization by the Americans. However, unlike the member countries of the European Union, the two countries have rarely acted as a bloc in seeking out third markets. On the contrary, the intense rivalry generated by this fight for a greater share of world exports has resulted in greater domestic protectionism. This is reflected in the rivalry for the rapidly expanding British market during the early part of this century, and the more current fight for emerging markets in Asia. It is possible that if bilateral agricultural disputes were not so consuming then perhaps Canada and the U.S. could act more aggressively as a hemispheric bloc to regain export losses (mostly to the EU) in growing import markets.

Third, when the North American economic environment has been relatively prosperous, the bilateral relationship between the two countries has been characterized by greater openness, which has in turn produced rapid growth in bilateral trade. This was certainly the case in the pre-Confederation era as well as during the post-World War Two era. Conversely, when the economic climate has been stagnant, as it was during the interwar years and during the recessions of the 1980s and early 1990s, the bilateral relationship has been characterized by protectionism and dispute, and the bilateral relationship, in both political and economic terms, has suffered.

It is clear from this analysis that both internal and external constraints have fundamentally shaped the bilateral trading relationship over time. The nature of this relationship is not likely to change in the immediate future. Indeed, the domestic political atmosphere in both countries has consistently derailed any recent efforts to strengthen the trading relationship as is evidenced by the 1994 bilateral wheat war (Alston, Gray, and Sumner 1994).

In a prior review of more recent bilateral difficulties in agricultural trade, the conclusion reached was that agriculture remains a highly subsidized and protected industry despite efforts at liberalization at the multilateral and regional levels (Marchildon and Noble 1991). Moreover, the Canada-United States Free Trade Agreement (CUFTA) of 1989, and the successor NAFTA of 1994, did not alter the basic trajectory of growing agricultural trade disputes between the two countries. As long as export and producer subsidies in Europe and North America encourage production above world demand, there will continue to be tension between the two countries as they struggle for market share in third countries. In addition, both countries will regard each other's subsidy, support, and marketing structures with suspicion, and deploy domestic trade laws against each other, although they will increasingly appeal to WTO dispute resolution mechanisms in place of the NAFTA/FTA mechanisms.

NOTES

I am grateful to Christopher Adams for his research assistance, without which it would have been impossible to write this article.

1. According to Shannon, the Canadian-born population in the United States increased from 250,000 in 1860 to 1,180,000 by 1900. Although a share of this number can be attributed to French-Canadians who moved to the textile towns of New England, a significant percentage was moving to take advantage of the only fertile agricultural frontier then being opened in North America (1959, 47).

2. Between 1901 and 1915, 930,000 Americans migrated to Canada from the United States (U.S. Bureau of the Census and Statistics Canada, *Migration between the United States and Canada*, 1990).

3. According to Fowke, the Empire preference of 2 shillings a quarter (approximately 6 cents a bushel) of wheat probably had little impact, given that the British Empire and Commonwealth countries together formed a wheat surplus area, but the issue of trade diversion has never been properly studied (1957, 260).

REFERENCES

Alston, J., R. Gray, and D. Sumner. 1994. "The Wheat War of 1994." *Canadian Journal of Agricultural Economics* 42: 231-51.

Bothwell, Robert, and John English. 1977. "Canadian Trade Policy in the Age of American Dominance and British Decline, 1943-1947." *Canadian Review of American Studies* 8: 52-65.

Cohn, Theodore H. 1990. *The International Politics of Agricultural Trade: Canadian-American Relations in a Global Agricultural Context.* Vancouver: University of British Columbia Press.

Doern, G. Bruce, and Brian W. Tomlin. 1991. *Faith and Fear: The Free Trade Story.* Toronto: Stoddart.

Drummond, Ian, and Norman Hillmer. 1989. *Negotiating Freer Trade.* Waterloo: Wilfrid Laurier University Press.

Evans, John W. 1971. *The Kennedy Round in American Trade Policy: The Twilight of the GATT?* Cambridge: Harvard University Press.

Fausold, Martin. 1990. "President Hoover's Farm Policies, 1929-1933." In Melvyn Dubofsky and Stephen Burwood, eds., *The Great Depression and the New Deal.* New York: Garland.

Fornari, Harry. 1976. "U.S. Grain Exports: A Bicentennial Overview." *Agricultural History* 50: 137-50.

Fowke, V.C. 1957. *The National Policy and the Wheat Economy.* Toronto: University of Toronto Press.

Granatstein, J.L. 1985. "Free Trade between Canada and the United States: The Issue that Will Not Go Away." In Dennis Stairs and Gilbert Winham, eds., *The Politics of Canada's Relationship with the U.S.* Toronto: University of Toronto Press.

Hamilton, W.E., and W.M. Drummond. 1959. *Wheat Surpluses and Their Impact on Canada-United States Relations.* Washington: Canadian-American Committee, National Planning Association.

Hart, Michael. 1996. *Damned If You Do and Damned If You Don't: The Trials and Tribulations of Canada-U.S. Agricultural Trade.* Occasional Papers in International Trade Law and Policy, No. 38. Ottawa: Carleton University.

Kottman, Richard. 1975. "Herbert Hoover and the Smoot-Hawley Tariff: Canada, A Case Study." *Journal of American History* 62: 609-36.

MacGibbon, D.A. 1952. *The Canadian Grain Trade, 1931-1951.* Toronto: University of Toronto Press.

Marchildon, Gregory P., and Vivian Noble. 1991. "Canada-U.S. Relations in Agricultural Trade: A Review of Recent Difficulties." *Canada-U.S. Outlook* 2: 3-19.

Marr, W., and D. Paterson. 1980. *Canada: An Economic History.* Toronto: Gage.

Officer, L.H., and L.B. Smith. 1968. "The Canadian-American Reciprocity Treaty of 1855 to 1866." *Journal of Economic History* 28: 598-623.

Pasour, E.C. 1990. *Agriculture and the State: Market Processes and Bureaucracy.* New York: The Independent Institute.

Rothstein, Morton. 1960. "America in the International Rivalry for the British Wheat Market, 1860-1914." *Mississippi Valley Historical Review* 47: 411-18.

Shannon, Fred. 1959. *The Farmer's Last Frontier: Agriculture, 1860-1897.* New York: Rinehart and Company.

Taussig, F.W. 1967. *The Tariff History of the United States.* New York: August M. Kelley.

U.S. Bureau of the Census and Statistics Canada. 1990. *Migration Between the United States and Canada.* Washington and Ottawa: U.S. Bureau of the Census and Statistics Canada.

Widdis, Randy. 1997. "American-Resident Migration to Western Canada at the Turn of the Twentieth Century." *Prairie Forum* 22: 237-62.

The Grain Trade in Contemporary Canada-U.S. Relations

RICHARD GRAY and MEL ANNAND

Background

Canada and the United States share the largest trading relationship between two sovereign nations that has ever existed. Much of current volume in trade has been the result of the tremendous growth subsequent to the 1989 Canada-U.S. Free Trade Agreement (CUFTA). Despite these very large commercial ties across many sectors, and the existence of NAFTA and World Trade Organization (WTO) agreements that outline rules for trade, trade in the grain sector has, nonetheless, been a frequent source of disputes. Increased grain exports from Western Canada into the U.S. have led to numerous disputes in which the U.S. government has legally challenged this Canadian access to its market.

This paper analyzes the economic and legal factors that have contributed to these recent grain trade disputes and, further, it speculates as to whether these factors will continue to create pressure for grain disputes. To these ends, it will begin with a brief review of the recent changes in the legal framework for Canada-U.S. trade as a result of CUFTA, NAFTA, and WTO trade agreements, and a description of some of the visible changes in the marketplace, including changes in the grain trade flows that have occurred in the last decade through the merger of firms. This will be followed by an analysis of the economic forces that have affected the Canada-United States grain trade and a description of some of the concerns of the U.S. industry with respect to grain exports from Canada. The final section of the paper contains our assessment of the likelihood of future grain trade disputes.

For many years there were significant barriers to trade in grains between Canada and the United States. Canada protected its domestic market for wheat, oats, and barley with the use of import licenses administered by the Canadian Wheat Board (CWB). This protection allowed the CWB to operate the "two-price policy," where CWB sales to domestic processors were generally maintained well above world prices. Until 1989, the United States had an import tariff of $0.21 per bushel ($8/t) on grain and canola that had not obtained GRAS ("generally regarded as safe for human food consumption") status from the U.S. Food and Drug

Administration (U.S. International Trade Commission). These measures virtually eliminated profitable arbitrage opportunities for Canada-U.S. grain trade. In January 1989, the Canada-U.S. Free Trade Agreement made a new attempt to integrate the North American grain market. It contained a formula to allow for removal of the Canadian import licenses and the U.S. import tariff on grains, eliminated export subsidies between the two grain markets, reduced Canada's grain transportation subsidy to some U.S. destinations, and obliged the Canadian Wheat Board (CWB) not to sell grain into the U.S. below cost. The most noteworthy aspect of CUFTA was that, for the first time, an international legal institution was created for the resolution of trade disputes between Canada and the U.S.: the Chapter 18 Binational Panel system. This new element of the legal trade framework was soon tested in the durum case we will turn to presently, but the system functioned effectively to bring a rules-based solution to a trade irritant. The application of the rule of law in an international setting, where power politics previously determined the outcome, was a welcome development for trade liberalization.

Since the agreement came into force, the United States has imported significant amounts of bread wheat, durum wheat, feed wheat, barley, oats, canola, and flaxseed. As shown in Figure 1, Canadian grain exports to the United States have risen steadily to exceed four million tonnes in the

Figure 1:   Canadian Grain Exports to the United States,
            1978-79 to 1996-97

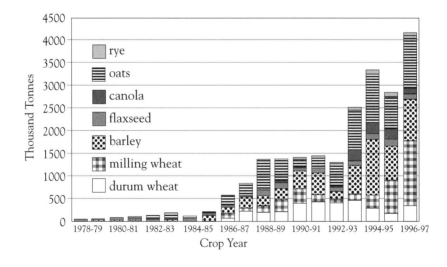

1996-97 crop year. What is most striking about the number is that both CWB grains (wheat and barley) and non-CWB grains (oats, canola, and flaxseed) have increased significantly since the CUFTA. The domestic sale of milling wheat, durum, and malting barley in Canada and the U.S. now takes place within a single market. The open border for grains has meant that non-CWB grains are traded freely both ways across the Canada-U.S. border. For CWB grains, the ability of Canadian firms to freely import U.S. product has meant that the CWB has adopted a domestic price that reflects the cash U.S. prices on a daily basis. The farm prices in Canada can, however, differ from U.S. cash market prices. While there are no U.S. restrictions on grain exports from Canada, the grain marketing system in Canada gives the CWB monopolistic control of wheat and barley exports from Western Canada, and the Ontario Wheat Marketing Board (OWMB) is the sole marketer of the small quantity of wheat produced in Ontario. Both the OWMB and the CWB operate annual price pools. Producers receive an average pooled price of domestic and export sales, which can differ from the daily North American domestic sale prices.

In addition to these trade effects, there has also been a considerable restructuring of the ownership of input supplier and grain marketing and processing firms in both Canada and the United States. Buschena and Gray (1997) show that the malting industry was dominated by five firms in the U.S. and four firms in Canada prior to CUFTA. These firms have merged or created joint ventures to form five firms, each with plants in both Canada and the U.S. The milling industry has shown a similar pattern of North American mergers. Large U.S. grain handling firms have also expanded into the Canadian grain handling business.

The shipments of grain from Canada became a major trade irritant to the United States, with legal disputes concerning the commodity beginning almost immediately after the CUFTA was implemented. Since 1989, there have been four significant legal challenges attempting to restrict Canadian wheat imports into the U.S. First, starting in 1989, North Dakota durum wheat producers argued that Canadian freight subsidies constituted an export subsidy, in violation of CUFTA Article 701.2. Second, after the United States Trade Representative determined that Canada had not violated this article (because the freight subsidy under the Western Grain Transportation Act applied to all shipments to Thunder Bay, whether destined for export or domestic use), the U.S. Congress instructed the International Trade Commission (ITC) to examine the "conditions of competition" between the U.S. and Canadian durum industries. The ITC rejected the argument that the CWB had been "dumping" durum into the United States (that is, selling into the U.S. below acquisition price). The third legal challenge was the case of Canadian durum wheat sales heard before the binational panel in 1992 under Chapter 18 of the CUFTA. The binational panel made its unanimous final ruling in early 1993, finding there was no compelling evidence that the CWB was selling below its acquisition cost.

On 1 January 1994, the North American Free Trade Agreement (NAFTA) came into effect. NAFTA adopts the CUFTA provisions affecting the Canada-U.S. grain trade and does little more. There is a separate Canada-Mexico agreement, but it is insignificant on grain matters. The main effect of the NAFTA has been to leave future trade liberalization to the multilateral arena of the World Trade Organization (WTO). Pending such future liberalization, domestic protection measures will continue to apply, subject only to the narrow limitations of the 1988 CUFTA.

Ironically, the fourth recent grain dispute case started in late October 1993, when the critical vote on NAFTA was before the U.S. House of Representatives. President Clinton wrote formally to key congressmen (who had tied their support for NAFTA to the wheat industry), pledging to investigate and possibly apply a Section 22 Agricultural Adjustment Act (AAA) action against Canadian wheat. After the successful NAFTA vote in late 1993, the U.S. administration resisted initial pressure to make an emergency Section 22 declaration and tried to ignore the issue altogether. However, in January 1994, the U.S. administration initiated a full ITC investigation under Section 22. President Clinton directed the ITC to investigate whether wheat, flour, and semolina imports "are being, or are practically certain to be, imported into the United States under such conditions or in such quantities as to render or tend to render ineffective, or materially interfere with, the price support, payment and production adjustment program conducted by the Department of Agriculture for wheat" (U.S. International Trade Commission Appendix).

In the ITC decision there were three separate reports to the president, each of which had distinct findings and recommendations. In one report, three of the six commissioners (including the Chair and Vice Chair) reported, as a group, that they determined that there was no "material interference" with the U.S. wheat program by imports. These commissioners, however, did provide the president with recommended import restraints should he determine, contrary to their findings, that there were grounds for restricting imports. A fourth commissioner determined that there was sufficient evidence to find material interference, but recommended only that a 10 percent additional duty be applied after imports reached 500,000 tons for durum and 800,000 tons for other wheat. Such a policy would not likely have had any significant impact on imports. The last two commissioners also found material interference and recommended that relatively tight tariff rate quotas be applied.

Before the president took any action relative to the Section 22 of the AAA case, the wheat trade dispute between Canada and the United States came to a negotiated resolution for the 1994-95 crop year. At the end of July 1994, the government of Canada agreed to limit wheat exports to the United States and the United States agreed to drop its efforts to secure an Article XXIII action under the GATT to restrict wheat imports. In an effort to find long-term solutions, the two states agreed that a binational commission of six to ten nongovernment experts be appointed to examine all aspects of Canadian and U.S. marketing and support systems and competition in third markets for wheat. The commission filed its final report in October 1995.

Under the "wheat peace" agreement, Canada was allowed to export 300,000 tonnes of durum and 1,050,000 tonnes of "other wheat" from the CWB region to the United States during the Canadian 1994-95 crop year at the existing NAFTA tariff rates. Shipments of durum between 300,000 and 450,000 tonnes were subject to $23 per tonne tariff. Shipments over 450,000 tonnes of durum and 1,050,000 of other wheat were subject to a more prohibitive $50 per tonne tariff. Shipments of soft winter wheat from Ontario and shipments of flour and semolina were exempt from any quantitative restrictions or additional tariffs. The agreement lasted for twelve months, ending in September 1995. No new agreement has been put in its place. During the one-year agreement, Canada exported 295,000 tonnes of durum and 950,000 tonnes of other wheat, but many speculate that these restraints had little influence on Canada-U.S. trade.

On 15 April 1994, the U.S. and Canadian governments signed the new WTO/GATT Agreement. Thus, as of January 1995, both states agreed to new tariff schedules for agriculture and, perhaps more significantly for the Canada-U.S. wheat trade, the U.S. gave up its AAA Section 22 rights and any existing quotas initiated under that act, all of which had been grandfathered under previous GATT agreements. The most significant development in the changing legal framework for the grain trade was the creation of the WTO in 1994. This supranational institution brought rule-based dispute resolution to agricultural trade for the first time. The Agreement on Agriculture contained commitments on reduction of export subsidies and domestic support programs, and this started a process of trade liberalization that will be continued in future negotiations. It has affected domestic policies (the elimination of Canada's WGTA subsidy) as well as border policies (tariffs and tariffication of quotas). International trade law will increasingly affect domestic policy choices as a result of the WTO agreements.

These new WTO trade rules are subject to a new legal system of dispute resolution involving mandatory consultations, impartial binding panel decisions, and an appeal process. The system operates within strict time limits that make it efficient and relevant to the parties involved. Future grain disputes between Canada and the U.S. will likely be resolved in this legal system. Grain trade issues are no longer subject only to national law, but are now also affected by international rules. The fact that these rules are part of a permanent multilateral institution means that they are a lasting step towards global free trade in grain.

Since the Section 22 hearings of 1994 there have been no significant grain disputes between Canada and the United States. No cases have been brought to the NAFTA or WTO trade panels. The only trade action of significance was the U.S. introduction of an End-use Certificate (EUC) for wheat imported into the United States early in 1995. Even this requirement turns out to have a very modest effect on trade flows and, according to Buckingham and Gray (1996), may have assisted Canadian producers by contributing to the CWB's monopoly control over wheat exports. Despite the lack of any tangible trade actions, the anti-Canadian grain trade rhetoric has continued in the United States. The U.S. Trade Representative, farm leaders, and congressmen from wheat-producing states have continued to publicly condemn Canada-U.S. grain trade and, in particular, the actions of the CWB. While expressing some frustration with the inability to discipline the actions of the CWB within the current trade agreements, these grain interests have made it very clear that they want to deal with the CWB within a larger context of State Trading Enterprises at the next round of the WTO, scheduled to commence in 1999.

Economic Forces that Have Affected Trade

CUFTA created a reduction in tariffs and, more significantly, secured Canadian access to the U.S. market, which created the ability to export grain when arbitrage opportunities warrant it. There have been numerous studies that have examined the economic forces that have increased Canadian grain exports to the U.S. Perhaps one of the most surprising outcomes of North American trade liberalization was the increase in Canadian grain shipments to the U.S. If the U.S. is a consistent source of production and export of wheat, coarse grains, and oilseeds, what factors made it profitable to ship grain to the United States rather than to ship it abroad? After all, on first blush this trade flow would appear to be one equivalent to "carrying coals to Newcastle." On the face of it, this counterintuitive trade flow may have raised the suspicion of those working in U.S. industry with respect to the profitability of such a move which, in turn, led them to investigate the possibility of Canadian dumping into the U.S. market. Several factors have been identified as potentially contributing to the profitability of exporting Canadian grain to the United States. Included in this list are the U.S. Export Enhancement Program, Canadian transportation subsidies, higher grain handling costs in Canada, the differentiated nature of wheat, a diversification of supply by some U.S. processors, shifts in comparative advantage, dumping by the CWB, and a lack of price transparency (giving an unfair advantage to the CWB in the U.S. market). Most of these factors have been examined in some detail.

Several studies have identified the Export Enhancement Program (EEP) as a strong factor contributing to an increase in trade flows. Schmitz, Gray, and Ulrich (1993), Wilson and Johnson (1995), and Schmitz and Koo (1996) identified EEP as a major factor in barley shipments. Sumner, Alston, and Gray (1994), Alston et al. (1997), and Gray and Gardner (1995), identified EEP as a major factor in increased wheat shipments. As a total these papers provide convincing evidence that EEP contributed to the increase in Western Canadian grain shipments to the U.S. The logic used in these studies was consistent: the EEP bonuses, which are a subsidy paid to grain exporters, drive a wedge between the U.S. domestic price and the price of grain in third-country export markets. These bonuses have at times exceeded $60 per tonne and have been used for over one-half of the barley, durum, and wheat exports. Faced with a third-country export price lower than the U.S. price, it became profitable for the CWB to ship grain to the U.S. In comparing Figure 2 with Figure 1 it is clear that, while the EEP may have contributed to the expansion of exports to the U.S., it is interesting to note that exports during the 1995-96 and the 1996-97 crop years exceeded 3.6 million tonnes, even though the EEP program was not used during these crop years. Thus, factors other than EEP must be contributing to the expansion of grain exports to the U.S.

The freight rate subsidy for the rail movement of grain in Canada has also been identified as a factor contributing to Canadian grain exports to the U.S. In fact, the freight rate subsidies to Thunder Bay were the basis of the 1989 CUFTA binational panel investigation. The subsidy was found to be consistent with CUFTA because it also applied to domestic shipments. In part due to budgetary pressures and in part due to the WTO, which limited the volume of grain that could be shipped under the WGTA, the government of Canada eliminated the WGTA in 1995. Ironically, subsequent economic analysis has shown that the effect of removing the Western Grain Transportation Act (WGTA) subsidy would be to increase shipments to the U.S. rather than reduce them. As Gray and Gardner (1995) point out, the removal of the subsidy WGTA makes the U.S. market more attractive than shipping to Canadian ports and could dramatically increase Canada-U.S. trade. Using the 1992-93 crop year and a point in southern Saskatchewan as a base, they indicate that the removal of the WGTA freight subsidy will increase the cost of shipping to any Canadian port by $22 per ton but will increase the cost of shipping to the U.S. at most by $8 per ton. This will generate even more pressure to ship to U.S. destinations.

Wilson and Johnson (1995) and Carter and Loyns (1996) have found that elevation and handling charges in the Canadian grain system

Figure 2: EEP Expenditures

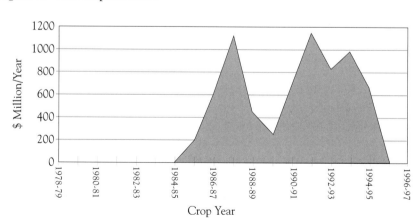

are greater than those found in the U.S. grain-handling system. Wilson and Johnson estimate that the primary and terminal charges in Canada total $33 per tonne compared to $16 per tonne in the U.S. They speculate that these lower U.S. costs are a result of a more rationalized grain-handling system that is better able to take advantage of economies of size in grain handling. They also suggest that subsidized rail freight rates in Canada have led to less pressure to reduce the grain-handling component of the costs. Carter and Loyns suggest that the cost difference is, in large part, due to the regulation of the Canadian grain system. It is also evident that the U.S. farm program subsidized both the construction and use of storage facilities and may have resulted in a greater overall capacity in the U.S. grain system, increasing the degree of competition in the sector. In Canada, the capacity at the west coast ports is still restrictive. These ports operate at nearly 100 percent of the capacity most of the time, which in turn reduces the pressures to compete for market share. Whatever the reason for lower grain-handling charges in the U.S., holding all other factors constant should contribute to increased grain exports to the U.S. If the port prices for grain are the same, then lower handling charges in the U.S. will increase the farm gate prices in the U.S., making delivery to those markets more economic than it would be otherwise.

Another factor that has been discussed is the notion that grains are differentiated products and that the U.S. may be deficient in grains with specific attributes, leading to a demand for imports from Canada. The notion of product differentiation becomes clearer when specific end uses are considered. For instance, barley can either be used as livestock feed or malted for the purpose of brewing beer. Within the varieties suitable for malting there are both two-row and six-row barleys. Six-row barley produces smaller kernels, giving the mash a higher fiber content and making it easier to add rice to the brewing process, while two-row barley has larger kernels, creating a higher beer yield per bushel. Six-row barley varieties are almost exclusively used in the U.S. domestic malting industry, whereas two-row varieties are sold to a small but growing portion of the domestic market and can be exported. The quantity of two- and six-row varieties suitable for malting can vary a great deal from year to year, depending on weather conditions. Disease, frost, drought, and rain during harvest can make a sample unfit for malting. Thus, while the U.S. may be in an export position for feed barley, they may be short of a specific type of malt barley. Equally, wheat and durum are also differentiated with respect to end use. Again, weather can play a large role in the availability of a specific type of wheat, making imports from Canada economic while other wheat types are being exported. This was apparent in 1993 when weather and disease damaged the U.S. durum wheat crop, creating a demand for Canadian product. As products become increasingly differentiated for specific end uses, the possibility of weather creating a regional shortage of product grows, which in turn increases trade flows.

Product differentiation also leads to two-way trade, even in years of adequate supplies, for reasons of managing supply risk. By establishing and maintaining long-term buying relationships with firms in different regions, a buyer is able to call on each of these suppliers for specific product types. This regional supply diversification is particularly important when weather can change the location where specific product types are produced. In the past these long-term relationships were often achieved through vertical integration of milling and brewing companies to establish buying facilities in several different regions. While Cargill has had a presence in grain handling in Western Canada since the 1970s, Archer Daniels Midland and ConAgra have also recently announced plans for expansion into Western Canada. Supply diversification can be accomplished through formal contracting of supplies in several regions. For example, Anheuser-Busch uses Saskatchewan Wheat Pool as an agent to contract with Canadian barley producers to grow a specific barley variety. In malting barley, bread wheat, and durum, supply diversification will mean increased exports from Western Canada, since most of the processing capacity is U.S.-based and often much of the high-quality supply can exist in Western Canada. For softer wheat processing facilities located in Eastern Canada, which traditionally relied on wheat produced in Ontario, supply diversification will mean establishing a greater tie with U.S. sources of supply and will result in greater imports from the U.S.

A third consequence of increasing product differentiation is that regional comparative advantage in producing specific product types can create regional specialization of production, resulting in greater trade. For example, canola oil has become increasingly differentiated from soybean oil. Because of its cool climate, Canada has a comparative advantage in the production of canola. As the U.S. consumer demand for this differentiated oil product has grown, the export of canola from Western Canada to the U.S. has increased dramatically—while the U.S. continues to be the world's largest soybean producer. There has been a dramatic increase in durum wheat production in Canada relative to the U.S., and an increase in durum exports to the U.S. In part this may represent a shift in comparative advantage. In the durum-producing regions of the U.S. (primarily North Dakota and Montana), semi-dwarf bread wheats have increased in yields, now yielding more than durum varieties. Given similar production costs, this means durum must sell at some premium relative to bread wheat to be economically competitive in the U.S. In Western Canada, where the growing season is very limited, bread wheats yield the same as durum wheat in many areas. This implies that the price of durum has only to equal spring wheat prices to compete economically. Given the premiums that have existed, the durum area has expanded in Western Canada. This expansion in Canada has, in turn, limited the premium for durum, which indirectly reduced the U.S. acreage.

There is also evidence that the recent increase in Canadian malting barley exports to the U.S. is also the result of some long-term comparative advantage. In Canada, most producers grow malting barley varieties. In 1994, 6.7 million acres or 60 percent of the barley area was planted to malting varieties (Schmitz et al. 1996). In a typical year, 20 to 30 percent of this barley would be selected for malting use, with the rest being sold into the feed market. Despite the low odds of receiving the malting premium, producers continue to grow malting varieties rather than feed barley because in most areas they yield the same amount per acre (Schmitz, Gray, and Ulrich 1993). In contrast, the selection rate for malting barley in the U.S. is typically 70 to 80 percent, and yet most producers choose to grow feed barley varieties to gain a yield advantage. The difference in selection rates suggests that in many years there is more quality malt barley available in Canada. This is consistent with the increase in malting barley exports from Canada to the U.S. from zero in 1989 to 721 million tonnes in 1994. Given the increased integration of the North American grain market, regional specialization of particular grain types is likely to be enhanced. To the extent that this specialization shifts production across the Canada-U.S. border, it will result in increased trade.

Several studies have examined the role of domestic farm income support policies on Canada-U.S. grain trade and concluded that, while these policies may have influenced producer incomes and production, they likely had little impact on trade. Gray and Gardner (1995) found that, since the 1985 U.S. farm policy has been largely decoupled, any production-enhancing effect of the policy would, in general, be more than offset by the acreage set-aside requirements. The Conservation Reserve Program (CRP) did reduce grain production and may have had some positive effect on grain prices. This effect would tend to raise both the U.S.

and the world price and would, therefore, have very little impact on Canada-U.S. exports. To the extent that grains are a differentiated product, the concentration of the CRP in some regions may have increased the U.S. import demand. In Canada, farm income support programs have also had a limited impact on production. The exception to this was the Guaranteed Revenue Insurance Program that operated from 1991 to 1992, which encouraged producers to seed more area. Since 1992, the farm income support has been limited to the Net Income Stabilization Account, which operates a subsided savings account for 2 percent of gross sales, and a Crop Insurance Program. Both of these programs provide a very modest amount of support and therefore have a modest positive effect on production. In addition, like the U.S. programs, the modest effect should be felt in both the world and U.S. markets and should, therefore, have very little impact on Canada-U.S. trade. Gray and Smith (1997) note that, in both Canada and the U.S., the overall level of support is decreasing and is being delivered in a less distortionary fashion; this suggests the limited effect that domestic policies have had and will likely continue to have on Canada-U.S. trade. The only caveat here is that if governments recover from their fiscal problems and grain prices fall considerably, the governments might respond with new farm-income support measures. These measures would be constrained by the WTO and, more importantly, governments are more likely to develop decoupled programs to minimize the impacts on production and trade. Thus, it is unlikely that domestic farm support measures will be the source of future grain trade disputes.

The Canadian Wheat Board was investigated for dumping into the U.S. market by the ITC in 1991 and by the binational CUFTA panel in 1992. Dumping is loosely defined as selling into another market at below the cost of acquiring a product. The investigations revealed that the CWB was selling into the U.S. market at prices above the initial price and, therefore, was not dumping. The results of the investigation are consistent with many studies that have found that, for much of the past decade, U.S. prices have been above the pooled prices in Western Canada (Carter 1995; Schmitz, Gray, and Ulrich 1993; Schmitz et al. 1996; and Wilson and Johnson 1995). The reason for this price premium in the U.S. market relative to the CWB pool return differs across studies. Alston, Gray, and Sumner (1994), Schmitz et al. (1996), and Schmitz, Gray, and Ulrich (1993) point out that the EEP program has to create a premium in the U.S. market relative to the world market, and the CWB did not flood the U.S. market in order to maintain access. The other reason for the price premium in the U.S. market is that the U.S. demand for Canadian wheat is relatively inelastic and that, by restricting sales to the U.S. and charging a premium price, the CWB can increase revenue. Finally, Carter (1995) argues that marketing costs in the Canadian system are so high that the U.S. prices remain at a premium to those observed in Canada.

A second concern related to dumping is the initial payment guarantee the CWB receives from the federal government. Because of the government guarantee, the level of the initial payments to the producer is established by order-in-council of the federal government. Since 1980 there have been a total of seven deficits in the four pool accounts, amounting to just over one billion dollars (Loyns and Kraut 1995). Some commentators have expressed concern because the level of the initial payment is set and guaranteed by the government of Canada, so that this policy instrument can be used as an income support measure to allow the CWB to effectively dump on the world market. The Canada-U.S. Joint Commission on Grain recommended that the CWB move to a commercially based initial payment system.

One of the major criticisms leveled at the CWB is the lack of price transparency, which gives the CWB an unfair advantage in selling grain into the U.S. market. These sentiments are reflected in the Canada-U.S. Joint Commission on Grains Report, which recommended that the CWB should become more price transparent. According to Wilson and Johnson (1995), there are many related concerns; however, the primary concern seems to be the inability of competitors to estimate at what price the CWB will make a sales offer. In the private grain trade, grain is procured in the country and sold at terminal or export markets. Given that cash country prices are easily established, the bid prices in the terminal markets will closely reflect these cash prices, so bids will occur in a narrow range. If the CWB is selling in the same market, there is no comparable cash or street price to estimate what the CWB price might be, whereas the CWB can easily estimate the private bid prices. This asymmetry of information is a point of concern for the U.S. industry and, thus, there have been many calls for price transparency on the part of the CWB. Wilson and Johnson point out that even the private trade is becoming far less transparent, as transportation rates differ by shipment and marketing firms contract farther ahead.

The Trade Issues from a U.S. Perspective

The American views on the CWB differ a great deal. It is clear from many public statements that, as long as the CWB is involved in the export of Canadian grain, the U.S. industry will suspect unfair behavior on its part. This is evident even by looking at the source of the disputes. Oat exports to the U.S. have increased as much as wheat, yet wheat has been the source of three different legal trade disputes, whereas oats have not been raised in any of the cases. The same can be said for canola. There is not, however, a one-to-one correspondence. Barley is marketed by the CWB, yet no trade disputes have arisen. In this case, the U.S. industry may recognize that Canada has large acreages of malting barley and that the CWB may have played a role in limiting the exports to the U.S.

Many studies have examined the impact of the increased Canadian exports on U.S. producer income. Some approaches have treated imports from Canada as new supply in the U.S. and found relatively large effects. For instance, in the Section 22 case USDA estimated a loss of twenty-two cents per bushel, due to increased imports during the early 1990s. Sumner, Alston, and Gray (1994), examining the same period, estimate that the increase in foreign demand created by the diversion of Canadian third-country export sales to the U.S. nearly completely offset the increased total U.S. supply. The net effect was less than one cent per bushel. The USITC used a Vector Auto Regressive model to estimate the relationship between supply and price and found a number halfway between the other two estimates. They assumed, however, that there would be no increase in third-country demand as a result of the diversion of Canadian exports to the U.S. In any case, there is a perception that Canadian exports reduce U.S. prices, which has contributed to the trade disputes. A more substantive claim is that the flow of Canadian grain often floods the grain handling and transportation system near the border, resulting in reduced access by U.S. producers. To the extent that Canadian shipments are unanticipated and to the extent that they move to primary elevator positions, such effects are real. But much Canadian grain goes directly to the end user, often via rail, and therefore does not congest the primary elevator system in any real way. As grain trade between the two countries becomes the norm, then, investments should follow that increase the capacity of the U.S. system along the border, such as the new handling facility built at Sweetgrass, Montana.

U.S. marketing firms, farm leaders, and politicians continue to raise the issue of "price transparency." Simply put, it is difficult for a U.S. firm to determine sale prices of the CWB—either before a sale is made or after the fact. According to Wilson and Johnson (1995), this gives the CWB an unfair advantage in marketing. Unlike most marketing firms that buy at one location and sell at another, the CWB pays producers an initial price and then offers to sell into many markets, attempting to maximize revenue. Because the CWB is assessing opportunities in many markets throughout the world, it is difficult for competitors to estimate at what price the CWB will offer to sell in the U.S. market. The CWB, on the other hand and as indicated above, can easily observe the cash prices in the U.S. and closely estimate what competitive bids will be. This transparency issue may diminish somewhat as these smaller players learn more about the new marketplace.

Price transparency is also an issue in international marketing. The CWB can make short-term sales concessions or undertake market development activities in order to build long-term trading relationships. This incentive to meet a customer's short-term needs for future considerations is a function of the volume of expected future business rather than monopoly powers. This puts smaller private firms at some disadvantage when they do not anticipate as much long-term business. Even though this CWB behavior may be a part of normal commercial practice, all firms would like to see the CWB curtailed in this ability. While these price discrimination practices may fall within the definition of normal commercial practices, they are a trade irritant from the U.S. perspective.

Conclusions

The NAFTA and the WTO guarantee Canadian access to the U.S. grain markets. The rules for trade are now clearly established and the dispute settlement process ensures some adherence to these agreed-upon rules of trade. This market access has allowed a significant growth in Canadian grain exports to the U.S. The increase in grain exports has helped U.S. grain processors and U.S. grain shippers but has had a limited negative effect on the income of producers, particularly those close to the Canadian border, and perhaps reduced the returns of smaller grain marketing firms. These perceived economic consequences have made grain exports from Canada an important political issue. The increase in Canadian grain exports to the U.S. has resulted in several grain trade disputes, all of which have dealt with durum wheat or bread wheat.

Given guaranteed access, market forces will continue to maintain, or even enhance, Canadian grain exports to the U.S. The open access to the U.S. market, combined with the elimination of the WGTA east-west freight subsidy, will make the U.S. an attractive market for differentiated grain products. Increasingly, U.S. grain processors will look to Canada as a means of diversifying sources of supply. Additionally, if the EEP were implemented again or freight rates were deregulated, even more pressure would develop for U.S. shipments. The operation of the CWB has been and remains the key trade issue. This is in part because the CWB is one of the few remaining differences between the Canadian and U.S. grain sectors and, thus, is being held accountable for increased trade flows. As long as the CWB is a part of these sales, the grain trade will continue to be a significant bilateral trade issue. However, it is not obvious that, if the CWB were eliminated and exports to the U.S. expanded, the U.S. wheat producers would not continue to mount opposition to Canadian wheat exports and look for other sources for dispute.

The ability of the U.S. industry to obtain remedies for CWB behavior seems remote within the existing NAFTA and WTO. State trading enterprises are allowed in the existing WTO and are allowed to price discriminate as long as they do so within the bounds of commercial practice. Price transparency and the conduct of state trading enterprises (STEs) will be examined in the mini-round of the WTO. Given the number of countries with STEs to protect, it is unclear whether discipline will be forthcoming in the next round and, if it is, it will likely be many years away. Therefore, the final decision concerning the CWB, at least in the short run, lies with Canadian wheat and barley producers and the Canadian government. The possibility that the domestic pressure for reform will cause the government of Canada to unilaterally remove the CWB also seems somewhat unlikely any time soon. A recent barley plebiscite showed that 62 percent of producers were in favor of retaining the CWB. Proposed amendments to the CWB Act will give producers more control of the CWB and may serve to stem some of the growing domestic opposition to the CWB.

On the U.S. side, Canada will be watching the use of the Commodity Credit Corporation and the Export Enhancement Program for breaches of the subsidy rules of international trade agreements. The U.S. Farm Bill and its farm support programs, although now largely decoupled from production, are still an irritant to Canadians in terms of the level of income support they give to American farmers. Despite larger volumes of Canada-U.S. grain trade, the number of future disputes will be relatively small. The disputes will involve some of the grain trade irritants listed above, with state trading the major current issue. Sanitary and biological issues will likely become the predominant issues of the future. There will be continued harmonization of standards between the two countries and this will keep the number of disputes to a minimum. However, given the apparent political influence held by grain trade interests in the U.S., there will always be grain trade disputes in one form or another. The disputes follow a familiar pattern of public posturing and subsequent legal processes. The NAFTA panel system will continue to be used, but the parties will now also have the WTO panel system available where appropriate. The WTO Agreement on Agriculture, and the possibility of future expanded reduction commitments on domestic and export subsidies, mean that more disputes in the grain trade are likely to be dealt with by the WTO as grain policies start to bump into the upper limits set by the WTO. The relatively quick dispute settlement process will encourage parties to use the WTO system.

It should also be recognized that, if a trade dispute is unresolved through the existing trade agreements, there will continue to be pressure for voluntary agreements, such as the Canada-U.S. Durum Agreement of 1994. Such agreements avoid the uncertainty, delay, and expense of the dispute resolution process. Despite the fact that such agreements reintroduce power-based rather than rules-based dispute resolution, the parties are attracted by the predictability of results. Therefore, voluntary agreements will continue to play a part in resolving trade disputes. Future trade negotiations will involve both bilateral and multilateral issues. In the NAFTA forum, these negotiations will focus on technical trade barrier issues, such as sanitary matters, and on subsidies. In the WTO forum, the issues will focus on the Agreement on Agriculture and further domestic and export subsidy reductions. State trading enterprises will also be discussed. Negotiations will take place against the background that Canada now offers little financial support to the grain trade, while the U.S. still spends billions on agricultural support. Canada will call on the U.S. to walk the free-trade talk.

REFERENCES

Alston, J., C. Carter, R. Gray, and D. Sumner. 1997. "Third-Country Effects and Second-Best Grain Trade Liberalization Policies: Export Subsidies and Bilateral Liberalization." *American Journal of Agricultural Economics* 79, no.4: 1300-1310.

Alston, J.M., R. Gray, and D.A. Sumner. 1994. "The Wheat War of 1994." *Canadian Journal of Agricultural Economics* 42: 231-51.

Buckingham, Donald, and Richard Gray. 1996. "North American Wheat Wars and the End-use Certificate—Compromising Free Trade?" Presentation to the Annual International Trade Research Consortium Meetings, December.

Buschena, David, and Richard Gray. 1997. *Trade Liberalization and International Merger in Cournot Duopolies: The Case of Barley Malting in North America.* Bozeman, MT: Northern Great Plains Trade Research Center.

Carter, C.A. 1993. *An Economic Analysis of a Single North American Barley Market.* Report prepared for the Associate Deputy Minister, Grains and Oilseeds Branch, Agriculture Canada. Ottawa.

Carter, C.A., and R.M.A. Loyns. 1996. *The Economics of Single-Desk Selling of Western Canadian Grain.* Edmonton: Alberta Agriculture, Food and Rural Development.

Carter, Colin. 1995. "Understanding the Canada/United States Grains Dispute: Factors and Impacts." In R.M.A. Loyns, Ronald D. Knutson, and Karl Meilke, eds., *Proceedings of the First Canada / U.S. Agricultural and Food Policy Systems Information Workshop.* Winnipeg: University of Manitoba.

de Gorter, H., and K.D. Meilke. 1987. "The EEC's Wheat Price Policies and International Trade in Differentiated Products." *American Journal of Agricultural Economics* 69: 223-29.

Gray, Richard, and Bruce Gardner. 1995. "The Impact of Canadian and U.S. Farm Policies on Grain Production and Trade." Prepared for a Workshop of the Canada / U.S. Joint Commission on Grains. New Orleans, 22-23 February.

Gray, Richard, and Vince Smith. 1997. "Convergence and Harmonization of Canadian and U.S. Agricultural Policies." *Canadian U.S. Agricultural Policy Harmonization.* Ottawa and Washington: Agriculture Canada and the United States Department of Agriculture.

Johnson, D., and W. Wilson. 1994. *North American Barley Trade Competition.* Agricultural Economics Report No. 314, North Dakota State University.

Johnson, P.R., T. Grennes, and M. Thursby. 1979. "Trade Models with Differentiated Products." *American Journal of Agricultural Economics* 61:120-27.

Kraft, D.F., W.H. Furtan, and E.W. Tyrchniewicz. 1996. *Performance Evaluation of the Canadian Wheat Board.* Winnipeg: Canadian Wheat Board.

Larue, B. 1991. "Is Wheat a Homogeneous Product?" *Canadian Journal of Agricultural Economics* 39:103-17.

Loyns, R.M.A., and Maurice Kraut. 1995. "Pricing to Value in the Canadian Grain Industry." *Canada - U.S. Joint Commission on Grains Final Report.* Ottawa: Agriculture and Agri-Food Canada.

Schmitz, A., R.S. Gray, T. Schmitz, and G.G. Storey. 1997. *The CWB and Barley Marketing: Price Pooling and Single-Desk Selling.* Winnipeg: Canadian Wheat Board.

Schmitz, A., R. Gray, and A. Ulrich. 1993. *A Continental Barley Market: Where are the Gains?* Saskatoon: University of Saskatchewan, Department of Agricultural Economics.

Schmitz, T., and W. Koo. 1996. *An Economic Analysis of International Feed and Malting Barley Markets: An Econometric Spatial Oligopolistic Approach.* Agricultural Economics Report No. 375, North Dakota State University, September.

Sumner, D.A., Julian Alston, and R.S. Gray. 1994. *A Quantitative Analysis of the Effects of Wheat Imports on the U.S. Market for Wheat, Including the Impact of Deficiency Payments.* Report for the Canadian Wheat Board for presentation to the U.S. International Trade Commission.

United States International Trade Commission (USITC). 1994. "Wheat, Wheat Flour and Semolina: Investigation No. 22-54." Publication 2794. Washington: USITC, July.

Wilson, W.W. 1989. "Differentiation and Implicit Prices in Export Wheat Markets." *Western Journal of Agricultural Economics* 14: 67-77.

Wilson, W.W., and P. Gallagher. 1990. "Quality Differences and Price Responsiveness of Wheat Class Demands." *Western Journal of Agricultural Economics* 15: 254-264.

Wilson, William W., and Demcey Johnson. 1995. "Understanding the Canada / United States Grains Dispute: Background and Description." In R.M.A. Loyns, Ronald D. Knutson, and Karl Meilke, eds., *Proceedings of the First Canada / U.S. Agricultural and Food Policy Systems Information Workshop.* Winnipeg: University of Manitoba.

Young, Robert E., II, Gary Adams, and Michael Helmar. 1995. "Effects of EEP on Canadian / United States Wheat Trade." In R.M.A. Loyns, Ronald D. Knutson, and Karl Meilke, eds., *Proceedings of the First Canada / U.S. Agricultural and Food Policy Systems Information Workshop.* Winnipeg: University of Manitoba.

U.S. Perspectives on Grain Trade with Canada: A Critical Appraisal

DEMCEY JOHNSON

Introduction

Grain trade presents a number of contentious issues for the United States and Canada. While both countries are traditionally net exporters, the United States has imported large amounts of Canadian wheat and barley in recent years—to the consternation of many U.S. producers. Differences in market organization between the United States and Canada and changes in the policy environment for agricultural trade have left plenty of room for public confusion about the causes of U.S. grain imports and whether anything can be done about it. This paper presents a summary and critique of U.S. perspectives on the "Canadian grain problem." To be clear, it is the wheat and barley producers in northern-tier states (and their congressional representatives) who are most concerned about Canadian grain imports. While other U.S. groups have a stake in the evolution of continental grain trade—specifically, millers, maltsters, grain merchants, and their trade associations—these are overshadowed in public discourse and political influence by the concerns of grain producers. Hence, much of this critique is addressed to the perceptions (and misperceptions) of U.S. wheat and barley producers and their political advocates.

Popular Views of the Canadian Grain Problem

Some complaints by U.S. producers are misguided. An example is the assertion that Canadian producers reap an unfair advantage because of the exchange rate. It is true that changing exchange rates can shift the competitive advantage between countries. However, a Montana farmer's letter to the Joint Commission on Grains (included in Volume II of its Final Report) reveals misunderstanding on a more basic level: "A Canadian farmer told me last week that the price of a bushel of wheat in Canada and here were comparable, but if he sold it down here he could get a 35% premium because of money differences. In other words, I sell my wheat and I get $3.50 per bushel. The Canadian dumps his load in the same pit with mine and he gets 35% more, or $4.77 in his money." To the Montana farmer, it appeared that "money differences" led to a higher return for his Canadian counterpart. (Presumably, part of the problem is that Canadians stubbornly refuse to change the name of their currency. If the Canadian farmer earned 4.77 *loonies* instead of *dollars*, the U.S. farmer would worry less about being cheated.)

From an economic perspective, what matters is changes in exchange rates and how these are passed through to costs of goods and services, rather than the levels of exchange rates per se. When the Canadian dollar loses value (depreciates), as it did during 1992-94 and most spectacularly during 1998, Canadian goods become more competitive in U.S. and offshore markets. But, at the same time, the Canadian farmer's depreciated dollar buys him less. Although Canada's competitive position has been enhanced by currency depreciation, this is properly viewed as a result of market forces. In an era when most governments (including Canada's) do not directly control their exchange rates, the "fairness" of currency fluctuations for U.S. producers is not really at issue.[1]

One of the most widely repeated, but (as yet) unsubstantiated, claims is that Canada unfairly subsidizes its grain exports to the United States. This is an almost reflexive allegation—that is, a "knee-jerk" one—by some U.S. farmers and politicians. It seems to stem from the identification of the Canadian Wheat Board (CWB) as a state trading enterprise and the conviction that the CWB does not "play fair" in international competition. Farmers are also perplexed by the fact that the United States imports any wheat. After all, one-half of the U.S. wheat crop is typically exported; why should a surplus producer be importing grain from Canada? Answer: It must be subsidized. In fact, "subsidies" are a slippery concept, admitting different interpretations and means of measurement (Huffbauer and Erb 1984, 9-13). For purposes of the Canada-United States Free Trade Agreement (CUFTA), trade negotiators agreed to use aggregate measures of producer subsidies (called "producer subsidy equivalents" or PSEs) as a trigger for trade liberalization in the grain sector. PSEs were initially higher in the United States, which allowed Canada to delay eliminating its license requirements for wheat and barley imports. There is a residue of unhappiness among U.S. wheat and barley producers about CUFTA, which they argue was too favorable to Canada—specifically, in how subsidies were measured, and what was left out of the agreement (North Dakota Barley Council 1997). However, historical measures show broadly similar levels of support for wheat and barley farmers in the two countries.

A related issue concerns the "dumping" of Canadian grain on U.S. markets. Evidence of dumping would be critical to U.S. producers seeking relief from imports. As normally defined, this means selling below the cost of production (or acquisition) and transport. By that standard, CWB would clearly be dumping if it sold wheat in U.S. markets at less than the initial payment paid to producers plus cost of handling and transport. To date, there has been little evidence of dumping by Canada (Gray and Annand 1998). Claims of "unfair subsidies" are less specific and therefore hard to prove or disprove. However, there is not much evidence of consistent underpricing by the Canadian Wheat Board. A 1990 International Trade Commission (ITC) investigation of durum found "no consistent price difference between prices of U.S.-grown durum and imported Canadian durum" (USITC 1990, ix). A 1994 ITC investigation of Canadian wheat, wheat flour, and semolina entering the U.S. market did lead to import restrictions under Section 22 of the Agricultural Adjustment Act. But Section 22 was invoked because imports caused "material interference" with USDA commodity programs, not because of Canadian subsidies. The ITC conducted price comparisons for U.S. and Canadian wheat offered to U.S. millers. They found that Canadian wheat was priced below U.S. wheat in twenty-eight of sixty-three instances, with margins as large as 12.8 percent. But Canadian wheat was priced *above* U.S. wheat in thirty-three instances, with margins as large as 20.0 percent (USITC 1994, II-79). Making direct comparisons is difficult on an ongoing basis because of the paucity of Canadian price data. There are also differences in quality—real or perceived—between "comparable" U.S. and Canadian grades, and buyers may have unique contract specifications that raise or lower their costs relative to standard grades. Economists like to assume that "wheat is wheat"—in our jargon, a "homogeneous" commodity—because that simplifies our analysis, but millers and grain traders know better.

Some claims of U.S. producers are basically correct, but practically irrelevant in the new trade policy environment. An example is the assertion that imports of Canadian grain depress U.S. grain prices and reduce farmer income. American farmers know this, as do their political representatives. It is an example of the "law of demand" at work: as larger quantities enter the market, prices are bound to fall. Economists put numbers to this idea using a "demand elasticity." Unfortunately, different statistical models (and data sets) produce different estimates, and there is little agreement about relevant elasticities—and hence about the impact of imports on U.S. grain prices. Several studies have been published with different conclusions about these aggregate effects (Gray and Annand 1998).

There are two complications to this line of analysis. First, utilization of wheat is divided into "food use" and "feed use" (for livestock feed). Different uses have different demand relationships. In general, imports of wheat for feed use are less likely to produce downward pressure on U.S. wheat prices. And much of the surge in U.S. imports from Canada in 1993-94 was accounted for by feed wheat. Second, U.S. imports of Canadian grain in the last decade have been induced, in part, by a U.S. program to subsidize exports. Under the Export Enhancement Program (EEP), the U.S. government offered subsidies for exports of wheat and barley to targeted markets. Higher U.S. exports raised domestic prices, while lowering prices in Canada's offshore markets. This created an incentive for Canada to shift exports to the U.S. market. In evaluating the impact of U.S. grain imports on prices, it is relevant to ask: Compared to what? If there had been no EEP, U.S. imports of Canadian grain would have been lower. With EEP in place, imports of Canadian grain are larger, and (estimated) price impacts are magnified. Whatever the "true" impact of grain imports on U.S. grain prices, this provides no legal basis for import restrictions. It was not always so. Section 22 was invoked to limit imports in 1995-96, but that authority lapsed with U.S. ratification of the WTO treaty. Nowadays, without changes to existing trade agreements, grain imports from Canada are just something U.S. farmers have to live with.

Substantive Issues in Bilateral Grain Trade

Several years ago, Canadian freight subsidies under the Western Grain Transportation Act (WGTA) were criticized for providing an unfair competitive advantage to Canadian grain producers. As it turned out, these U.S. criticisms were misplaced: with elimination of the WGTA subsidies in 1995, the higher cost of rail shipment to Canadian ports made southerly grain flows more attractive. Thus, eliminating subsidies induced a larger influx of Canadian grain into U.S. markets (Johnson and Wilson 1995). For U.S. producers this recalls the dictum: "Be careful what you wish for, because you may get it."

While WGTA subsidies (and their removal) were the focus of much debate and analysis at one time, other aspects of the Canadian transportation system are now coming under scrutiny—not least because of the discriminatory treatment accorded nonboard and non-Canadian grains. To put this in context, it should be noted that even after subsidy elimination, Canadian rail rates (for example, from prairie locations to ports) are substantially lower than the rates charged by U.S. carriers for similar movements. The lower Canadian rates reflect regulated rate structures. (These may change in the next several years as a result of regulatory review.) From a U.S. perspective, however, the critical point is that (comparatively) low Canadian rail rates apply legally only to grains grown in Canada (Wilson and Dahl 1998). This prevents U.S. grain shippers—especially those situated along the border—from taking advantage of low Canadian rail rates for transshipment of U.S. grain bound for the west coast. A second, overtly discriminatory feature is the system for allocation of railcars, which gives preferential treatment to the Canadian Wheat Board. Nonboard grains (including oats, canola, and any U.S. grains moving through the Canadian system) are residual claimants for railcars. This differs from the nondiscriminatory treatment given Canadian grain by U.S. rail carriers and may become a point of contention as pressures emerge for crossborder flows in both directions.

Another set of issues concerns pooling of freight costs for board grains. In Canada, all costs of marketing board grains (that is, transportation and handling) are aggregated and deducted from total sale revenue. Practically, the pooling of costs is inseparable from the pooling of sale prices, yet some implications of cost pooling are worth drawing out. Although transportation differentials figure into the final prices received by producers in different locations, these bear no necessary relationship to actual shipment patterns. Unlike in the United States, where values of grain adjust instantaneously to changes in sale prices and shipping costs, in Canada the pooling mechanism masks the values (costs and prospective returns) for individual transactions. And costs of "inefficient" grain movements are absorbed by all Canadian producers who sell through the board.

This is clearly viewed as a problem in Canada—concerns about systemic inefficiencies underlie the controversy about whether the CWB should retain its single-seller status[2]—but why should it matter to the United States? Three reasons are suggested. First, the pooling system facilitates shipment patterns that "make no sense" in terms of logistical efficiency, and would not be observed in a competitive marketing environment.[3] For U.S. observers, this adds to uncertainty about flows of Canadian grain and reinforces the view that the CWB is not bound by the same strictures as private grain-marketing firms. Second, with losses on individual transactions obscured through cost-averaging, it is harder to gauge the "fairness" of Canadian sale prices. (For that matter, it is hard for Canadian producers to know the value of their grain in terms of current sale opportunities.) Third, if marketing costs for board grains are inflated, the effect may be to accentuate the gap between U.S. and Canadian producer prices, creating greater incentive for crossborder arbitrage.

From the U.S. perspective, the basic questions are whether trade flows are distorted by various features of the Canadian system and whether U.S. grain producers are materially affected. These have political resonance (at least in the northern plains) and may be confronted in future trade negotiations, but are analytically difficult. Many features of the Canadian system are functionally inseparable. Thus, the railcar allocation system is designed to accommodate the Wheat Board, the pooling system is a requirement of single-desk selling, and grain delivery patterns (by producers to elevators) are constrained by the pooling system.[4] Disentangling these features and identifying their effects on trade is not easy.

The second area of contention is unequal market access. There is a common perception among U.S. producers that, despite some liberalization of trade under CUFTA, Canada has allowed limited access to its own grain markets. This is supported (at least superficially) by the fact that flows of wheat and barley have been overwhelmingly from Canada to the United States since CUFTA came into effect. The truth is a bit more complicated. Major trade barriers have been removed in Canada—specifically, import license requirements for wheat and barley, eliminated in 1995 under terms of the WTO agreement—but other, subtler features of the Canadian system can make it impractical to import U.S. grain.[5] Among these are requirements for end-use certificates, quality controls, and variety licensing.

When a Canadian buyer imports U.S. wheat for human consumption, the grain must be accompanied by an end-use certificate (EUC). This allows the U.S. wheat to be tracked to its final destination. En route, the U.S. wheat must also be segregated from Canadian wheat—ostensibly to avoid compromising Canada's system of grain quality controls.[6] These requirements raise handling costs (since segregation of U.S. grain requires extra bin space) and reduce opportunities for resale by Canadian buyers. Canadian imports of U.S. feed wheat must be "de-natured" (by coloring some percentage of kernels) to make the grain visually distinguishable from Canadian supplies. Imports of wheat and barley for seed use are allowed only for varieties that have undergone a rigorous testing and approval process—again, to preserve the integrity of Canada's grain quality system (USDA-FAS 1997, 43).

The Joint Commission on Grains, which was convened in 1994-95 to recommend solutions to the bilateral trade dispute, noted that Canada's system of variety controls was in conflict with the objective of achieving reciprocal market access. However, the commission recommended that Canada take action to provide nonregistered varieties (from U.S. and Canadian origins) with better access to Canada's handling and transportation system. The commission also recommended an end to EUC requirements in both countries (Canada-United States Joint Commission on Grains 1995, 94). To date, there has been little movement in this direction.

It may be argued that this is much ado about nothing. After all, the U.S. grain market is substantially larger than Canada's—nine times larger in terms of total cereal grain consumption—so that, even if remaining barriers to trade in Canada were removed, the overall tendency would be for grain to move from Canada to the United States. Problems of market access, from this viewpoint, are primarily important for symbolic reasons: they raise questions about the "fairness" of our bilateral grain trade. This is not to deny that northbound movements could make economic sense in some instances. For example, because of growth in its livestock sector (and rise in demand for feed barley), Alberta could cease to be a barley-surplus region in the next several years. Alberta feedlots might then import barley from Montana.

Ultimately, "market access" may be less significant for U.S. producers than access to Canada's handling and transportation system, particularly in view of the favorable rates on Canadian rail shipments. It bears repeating that, while U.S. rail carriers do not price their services differently for U.S. and Canadian grain, the Canadian rail carriers are not bound to provide U.S. grain with (low) regulated rates. Nor does U.S. grain have equal access (on nondiscriminatory commercial terms) to Canadian railcars or port facilities. The upshot is that U.S. grain producers cannot take advantage of the Canadian rail transportation system (for example, for shipments to the West Coast), but must bear the high costs of shipping by U.S. rail carriers. Meanwhile, Canadian grain has unfettered access to the U.S. grain handling and transportation system—as many North Dakota and Montana producers are aware, having encountered lines of Canadian grain trucks at their local elevators.

This latter image leads to what is perhaps, to U.S. minds, the most contentious ongoing issue of all: the role of the Canadian Wheat Board. The CWB lies at the center of U.S. complaints about our grain trade with Canada. Issues relating to state trading enterprises (STEs) have been elevated to the top of the USDA agenda for upcoming rounds of multilateral trade negotiations, in part because of continuing irritation over the

competitive advantages enjoyed by the CWB (Furtan and Baylis 1998).
What are these advantages? Unlike U.S. grain trading firms, the CWB
does not compete for grain procurement. Western Canadian farmers must
sell their wheat or barley to the board unless it is for domestic feed use.
This facilitates long-term marketing strategies and forward sales commitments, because the board has a lock on grain supplies. Downside protection is provided through the Canadian government's initial payment
guarantee. This is equivalent to price insurance and represents an implicit
subsidy whether or not the pool accounts wind up in deficit. U.S. trading
firms, in contrast, buy price protection by hedging in futures markets.
CWB borrowings are guaranteed by the government, so the board's interest
costs are low. What is more, the CWB pushes most costs of grain storage onto
Canadian producers; although it enjoys certain access to supplies, the CWB
takes ownership of the grain only at the time of delivery. To obtain the same
position, a U.S. firm would have to buy grain—and incur storage costs—
or hedge in futures markets—which also costs money.

The CWB can offer different prices to different buyers, a practice
known as "price discrimination." Defenders of the board hold this up as
the major advantage of single-desk selling. In principle, the CWB can
maximize sales revenue (net of shipping costs) by offering high prices in
some markets and low prices in other markets. Whether the board does a
good job of this has been the subject of much debate in Canada.[7] But what
does it mean for the United States? Economic theory provides some in-
sight. If the CWB allocates its sales optimally, theory suggests, it will sell
more grain to price-responsive markets and less to price-insensitive markets. A standard for comparison is competitive market equilibrium, where
selling prices (net of transport) are equalized across markets. If demand
in the United States is more price-sensitive than Canada's alternative
markets, then the CWB should direct more exports to the United States—
that is, more than what would occur under a competitive grain marketing system. And larger U.S. import volumes must depress U.S. prices.

But U.S. utilization of wheat is comprised of both food and feed use.
Suppose that Canada sends mostly food wheat to the United States. This
demand is less price-sensitive than the demand for feed wheat (which
depends on the price of corn and other substitutes). If, in addition, U.S.
demand for food wheat is less price-sensitive than offshore demand, the
preceding arguments are reversed: the CWB would direct a smaller volume of exports to the United States, compared to volumes that would
occur under competitive market conditions. In that case, the net effect

of the CWB's involvement is to raise U.S. prices, not lower them.[8] The point is that the ability of the CWB to practice price discrimination, per se, does not imply lowering of U.S. wheat prices.

The advantages associated with single-desk selling require that the CWB mask its terms of trade (prices, grain qualities, and payment terms). Pricing secrecy allows the CWB to extract large premiums in some markets, while selling at a discount elsewhere. Defenders of the board argue that it is not fundamentally different than private U.S. grain trading firms in terms of pricing disclosure: Cargill and Continental Grain do not divulge the terms of their transactions either. However, private U.S. firms have access to extensive market information, which allows them to develop refined judgments about the prices offered by their competitors. Canada does not have comparable market information—quoted values of board grains reflect pooled returns, rather than instantaneous trading pressures—and the CWB has considerable latitude in its selling prices because it does not compete for procurement. In short, there is an asymmetry between what Canada knows about U.S. grain prices and what U.S. firms know about Canadian prices. Arguably, this asymmetry works to the advantage of the CWB in bidding competition.[9] The so-called "transparency problem" is likely to remain a point of contention between the United States and Canada. It is symptomatic of the uneasy coexistence of our two marketing systems: one dominated by a monopoly seller, the other characterized by vigorous interfirm competition.

U.S. producer attitudes about the Wheat Board are decidedly mixed. CWB sales of wheat and barley into the United States (and some foreign markets) are viewed as pernicious. However, many U.S. producers envy the CWB's market power and marketing acumen and argue that they should have access to a similar institution—or that the board should be opened to both U.S. and Canadian grain. North Dakota's Republican governor, Ed Schafer, has suggested that chronic trade disputes could be resolved through "joint marketing" of U.S. and Canadian grain. His argument is that joint marketing would allow the United States and Canada to exert their combined market power and extract large price premiums, particularly in a commodity like durum wheat. Senator Byron Dorgan, a Democrat, also from North Dakota, one of the surest critics of "unfair" competition from the Canadian Wheat Board, has also voiced support for the joint marketing idea (*Forum* 1997), without proposing how this could be put into effect.[10] It may be argued that the U.S. Export Enhancement Program already vests something like single-desk selling powers in the U.S.

Department of Agriculture, at least for subsidized export sales. But, how hard would it be for U.S. program administrators to consult with Winnipeg before fixing EEP bonus levels? Not very, one reasonably assumes.

For various reasons, the joint marketing idea is probably a non-starter. Politically, there is little chance of any coordinated bilateral approach to state trading in grains. (The EEP program is now inactive and likely to remain so because of budgetary pressures.) The CWB is not authorized to market grains grown outside of Western Canada. And, while U.S. producers admire some aspects of the Canadian system, it is not clear that many would be willing to relinquish their right to make independent marketing decisions. They would like the right, but not the obligation, to sell through a pooling system—and many Canadian producers feel the same way.

To consider an entirely different question: Would U.S. producers be better off if the Wheat Board were divested of its legal monopoly? The answer is not obvious. Despite U.S. complaints, it is possible that the CWB has exercised restraint in exporting to the United States—more than could be expected from a liberalized Canadian market system—either because of missed opportunities (as some Canadian critics have claimed) or because of the political sensitivity of these trade flows. The case of oats is suggestive. The board lost its marketing authority for oats in 1989, and since that time U.S. imports of oats from Canada have steadily increased. However, this has not led to anything like the kind of public outcry that we have seen from U.S. wheat and barley producers. If the economic effects of eliminating the Wheat Board are uncertain, at least this would diffuse much of the public controversy and political posturing over U.S. grain imports.

Conclusions

With two radically different grain-marketing systems operating side by side, there are many sources of bilateral friction in the grain sector. The role of the Wheat Board has assumed great, and perhaps exaggerated, importance for U.S. farmers and policymakers. However, the huge difference in market size and other transitory economic factors are surely more important for explaining flows of grain from Canada to the United States. In several of its dimensions, the controversy over grain trade revolves around differences in regulatory regimes. These are hard to reconcile and pose questions for the United States just as they do for Canada. If Canadians enjoy relatively cheap rail transportation, that is because of Canada's regulated rate structure. The deregulation of U.S. rail rates in the 1980s, combined with the market power of U.S. rail carriers, may account for the high cost of shipping grain in northern-tier states. (In this, certainly, Canada is in no way implicated; we did this to ourselves.) But barriers to access, on the Canadian side, elevate the importance of differences in our rail transportation systems.

Contrasts are also evident in other areas, notably grain quality and variety licensing. In the United States, producers have more latitude in terms of variety selection, and grain handlers view quality assurance (for example, through cleaning and blending) as a commercial function, responsive to price incentives that vary across buyers through time. The Canadian system of quality assurance involves a much greater overlay of regulatory authority and restrictions (for example, varietal controls, required segregations within the handling system, and so on). To some degree, these restrictions limit the flow of U.S. wheat and barley into Canada. But while this represents a (relatively minor) trade irritant for the United States, Canada views its grain quality system as a source of competitive advantage in international markets. Thus, Canadians argue, it is unrealistic for Canada to subordinate its quality system (and export strategy) to the goal of reduced friction over continental grain trade. U.S. observers, for their part, need convincing that any differential treatment of U.S. grain within Canada is justified.

Two final points are in order. The first is that, with or without pressure from the United States, there is real evidence for change within Canada. As part of the ongoing reform of Canadian rail transportation, there will be a review of maximum freight rates in 1999. This could lead to complete deregulation of rail rates (which could make moot the issue of unequal access for U.S. grain) or other, more modest restructuring. The organization of the CWB is also under review. Among other things, the proposed amendment to the Canadian Wheat Board Act would give more flexibility to the CWB in its marketing operations, risk management, and how it compensates producers—in effect, allowing it to operate more like a commercial firm.[11]

The second point is that pressures for integration of the U.S. and Canadian grain sectors are coming from commercial sources—in particular, from companies with substantial investments (for example, in grain handling or processing facilities) on both sides of the border, or companies wishing to diversify their sources of supply. While interests of grain producers have dominated public discussions of trade issues, the interests of large agribusiness firms (ADM, ConAgra, Anheuser-Busch) will militate against trade barriers in either direction.

NOTES

1. Popular concerns about exchange rates are shared by some U.S. politicians. Senator Kent Conrad of North Dakota, in explaining his opposition to fast-track trade legislation, complained that other countries can devalue their currencies and thereby negate the effects of lower import barriers, leaving U.S. export firms no better off than before trade liberalization. Senator Byron Dorgan of North Dakota raised other objections to fast-track; as evidence of "soft-headed" U.S. trade policies, he cited the trade agreement with Canada and the resulting "flood of unfairly subsidized Canadian grain." Fast-track would expand the president's negotiating authority for international trade agreements. Under fast-track, the Senate cannot amend a proposed trade agreement but can only vote it up or down.

2. Carter and Loyns conclude that higher marketing costs more than offset whatever benefits accrue to Canadian producers from the CWB's single-seller status.

3. Consider the following example recounted by a U.S. observer. The CWB had committed to sell barley to an offshore (Pacific Rim) buyer, but faced bottlenecks in the Canadian rail system. Its solution was to ship barley by truck from as far north as Edmonton, Alberta, to Great Falls, Montana, where it was placed on U.S. rail for shipment to the West Coast. In doing so, the CWB incurred trucking costs of about twenty-five cents per bushel. It could have saved these costs (while fulfilling its export obligation) by buying U.S. barley in Great Falls. Instead, the extra trucking costs were absorbed by Canadian producers.

4. Producers throughout the Prairie provinces have equal access to pool accounts. Thus, when the CWB announces that it is accepting delivery for a given class of grain, producers can deliver at all locations. This ensures that all producers have timely access to the initial payment. However, the simultaneous delivery of grain to multiple locations is not necessarily efficient from the standpoint of transportation and logistics.

5. Canada stopped requiring import licenses for U.S. wheat in 1991. When the WTO agreement came into force, Canada converted its import license requirements into tariff-rate-quotas (TRQ). The under-access tariffs on barley were eliminated in January 1998.

6. In fairness, the United States also now requires end-use certificates (EUC) for imports of Canadian wheat. There are also some U.S. restrictions on commingling of U.S. and Canadian grain—specifically, to prevent Canadian grain from being exported under U.S. subsidy programs (EEP and GSM). This policy was introduced in response to Canadian EUCs, instigated by senators unhappy about inflows of grain from Canada, and over the objections of the U.S. grain trade.

7. Two studies favorable to the CWB are Kraft et al. (1996) and Schmitz et al. (1997). Carter and Loyns (1996) offer a contrasting view.

8. The earlier argument may still apply to trade in feed wheat. If the U.S. is a more elastic (price-sensitive) market than Canada's alternatives, CWB control should lead to higher exports to the United States. However, U.S. imports of feed wheat are somewhat episodic and do not seem to attract the same level of public concern.

9. The problem was more pronounced when the EEP program was active. EEP provided public disclosure of U.S. subsidy payments by importing country; from these, U.S. sale prices could be inferred with some precision.

10. Actually, the idea has a long history. Schmitz et al. (1981) developed economic arguments for an international wheat export cartel.

11. The 25 September 1997 news release announcing the amendment is posted at http://www.agr.ca/cb/news/n70925ae.html

REFERENCES

The Canada-United States Joint Commission on Grains. *Final Report*. Submitted to the U.S. Secretary of Agriculture and Canadian Minister of Agriculture and Agri-Food, October 1995.

Carter, C.A., and R.M.A. Loyns. *The Economics of Single Desk Selling of Western Canadian Grain*. Report prepared for the Associate Deputy Minister, Grains and Oilseeds Branch, Agriculture Canada, Ottawa, March 1993.

Conrad, K. "No Fast-Track Without the Three Cs." *Forum* (Fargo, ND) (13 November 1997): A4.

Dorgan, B. "Our Soft-Headed Trade Policies Should Not be On the Fast Track." *Forum* (Fargo, ND), Letter to Editor (28 September 1997): E7.

_____. "Joint U.S.-Canada Grain Strategy Makes Sense." *Forum* (Fargo, ND), Letter to Editor (4 November 1997).

Furtan, W.H., and K.R. Baylis. "State Trading in Wheat: Perceptions and Reality in Canada-U.S. Relations." *The American Review of Canadian Studies* 28 (1998): 287-313.

Gray, R., and M. Annand. "The Grain Trade in Contemporary Canada-U.S. Relations." *The American Review of Canadian Studies* 28 (1998): 253-71.

Hufbauer, G.C., and J.S. Erb. *Subsidies in International Trade* (Washington: Institute for International Economics, 1984).

Johnson, D.D., and W.W. Wilson. "Canadian Rail Subsidies and Continental Barley Flows: A Spatial Analysis." *Logistics and Transportation Review* 31 (1995): 31-46.

Kraft, D.F, W.H. Furtan, and E.W. Tyrchniewicz. *Performance Evaluation of the Canadian Wheat Board* (Winnipeg: Canadian Wheat Board, 1996).

North Dakota Barley Council. "Canadian Barley Trade: A Plethora of Distortions." *Barley Bulletin* 15 (1997): 1,7.

Schafer, E. "Joint Marketing a Workable Concept." *Agweek* 13 (17 November 1997): 4.

Schmitz, A., A. McCalla, D. Mitchell, and C. Carter. *Grain Export Cartels* (Cambridge: Ballinger Publishing, 1981).

Schmitz, A., R. Gray, T. Schmitz, and G. Storey. *The CWB and Barley Marketing: Price Pooling and Single-Desk Selling* (Winnipeg: Canadian Wheat Board, 1997).

United States Department of Agriculture, Foreign Agricultural Service. *Grain and Feed Annual Attache Report—Canada*. USDA-FAS, Washington, DC, 26 March 1997.

United States International Trade Commission. *Durum Wheat: Conditions of Competition Between the U.S. and Canadian Industries*. Report on Investigation No. 332-285 under Section 332(g) of the Tariff Act of 1930 as Amended, USITC Publication 2274, Washington, DC, June 1990.

_____. *Wheat, Wheat Flour, and Semolina*. Investigation No. 22-54, Publication 2794, USITC, Washington, DC, July 1994.

Wilson, W., and B. Dahl. *Reciprocal Access in U.S. / Canadian Trade: Background Issues for the U.S. Grain Trade*. Agricultural Economics Report, Department of Agricultural Economics, North Dakota State University, Fargo, 1998.

State Trading in Wheat: Perceptions and Reality in Canada-U.S. Relations

W.H. FURTAN and K.R. BAYLIS

Introduction

There are few topics that incite more emotion in Canada-U.S. economic discussions than the issue of unfair trade. Trade between the two countries has always been important because of its size and, in the past, major trading agreements such as the Auto Pact resulted in the development of a large-scale integrated North American industry. Given this, the trade in agricultural products has been limited because of tariffs and because the two countries compete for many products. Recent agreements such as the CUFTA and NAFTA have lowered the tariff and nontariff barriers between the countries but trade irritants, especially in agriculture, remain. Looking broadly, in the United States the existence and operations of the Canadian Wheat Board (CWB) raise a number of questions as to the fairness of Canadian trade in wheat (durum and bread wheat) and barley. In Canada, the operations of the Commodity Credit Corporation (CCC) and the presence of the Export Enhancement Program (EEP) make Canadians question whether the U.S. is a fair trader in grains. The problem is accentuated by the proximity of the two countries and because the grain-growing regions of both countries are separated by a border that is easily crossed. If the surplus grain regions were farther apart, such as those of North America and Europe, the problems would likely be of a different nature.

Part of the impetus for the grain dispute lies with the institutional differences in Canada and the U.S.; each country's institutions were born and grew out of different policy paths taken by the countries in developing their grain sectors. In the latter part of the nineteenth and early-twentieth century, the grain industry in both countries operated as an open and free market. At the end of the last century, regulations in Canada were being put in place that affirmed Canada as a grain-exporting nation. The Crow's Nest Pass Agreement (1897) in effect froze the freight rate on the export of grain from the prairies and, by the end of World War Two, the CWB was in place. By 1945-49 it was clear that Canadian farmers would be exporters of wheat and that the national market would always be small. In the U.S., the focus was on the domestic market. The government introduced a number of programs to support farmers but left the grain trade to the private sector. The U.S. started its loan rate and target price, crop insurance systems, and other programs as an attempt to support farmers in the domestic market (Tweeten 1970).

While the two countries started from a different trade orientation, today they compete in the export market. The institutions developed over time are different because of their historical roots, but today they clash. The important difference between the two countries lies not only in the institutions but also in the policies that the countries have adopted to deal with the grain trade. In view of this, the purpose of this paper is three-fold. First, we review some of the definitions of state trading and examine how state traders could affect trade between countries. Second, we review the recent history leading up to the U.S.-Canada wheat conflict and, finally, we discuss the perceptions of the key industry and government players about the wheat conflict and State Trading Enterprises (STEs).

Definition, Theory, and Magnitude of State Trading in Wheat

State trading is a broad term that has been used to cover many different kinds of government intervention in trade. The perception, and thus the definition, of state trading will vary between its purpose and effect. State traders can be defined by their policy objectives or through their influence on trade. Although it is primarily the effect of STEs, specifically their potential to distort trade, that raises concern amongst trading partners, it is the policy purposes of STEs that will be of key importance to their domestic masters. If the state is involved in some way in trade, it can be assumed that there is some direct or indirect policy objective that the state is attempting to fulfill. "State trading occurs when there exists a trading organization for which the prices and/or quantities of international transactions in commodities are determined as an instrument in the pursuit of the objectives of government policies" (Lloyd 1982, 119). If a state trader is setting prices and/or quantities, it does not necessarily imply that trade is shifting from what would occur under competition. One policy objective may, in fact, be to move the industry closer to a competitive equilibrium. As Simonot notes, "A general objective of many parastatals is the improvement of the functioning of a market or elimination of a market failure" (Simonot 1997, 12). Thus, the impact of an STE on trade will vary with the kind of market structure in which it is operating.

When governments set up state trading organizations to implement policy, they most often pass legislation that gives the organizations certain powers and it is these powers, and the way in which they are carried out, that is of greatest concern to trade partners. If the power given to the trader allows it to move from the competitive solution, then it has the ability to distort trade. Examples of this would be the granting of a monopoly or monopsony. For this reason, attention is given to the enterprises created or supported by governments to determine whether or not they are operating within the agreed rules of the GATT.[1] At the Uruguay Round, in the interpretation of Article XVII of the GATT 1994, state trading was defined as: "governmental and nongovernmental enterprises, including marketing boards, which have been granted exclusive or special rights or privileges, including statutory or constitutional powers, in the exercise of which they influence, through their purchase or sales, the level or direction of imports or exports" (United States General Accounting Office [GAO] 1996, 16). This would seem to imply that for a trader to be considered an STE, it must affect the quantity or flow of commodity traded.

The GATT requires three things from STEs. First, the STE must operate on nondiscriminatory treatment of trade (that is, different prices are charged for market reasons, not for political reasons). If state traders have a large degree of market influence, they may be able to buy or sell the same product at different prices from or to different markets. Although this distorts trade—that is, it moves away from a competitive equilibrium—it does not necessarily contravene international trade regulations. Price discrimination is not itself a GATT violation, provided it is only for commercial reasons (this will be discussed in more detail below). Second, the GATT requires that the use of quantitative restrictions is to be limited. Economists agree that tariffs are often more efficient and easier to lower over time than quantitative restrictions. Third, information about the STE and its operations is to be regularly provided to the GATT (Baban 1977).

With respect to the third requirement, the World Trade Organization (WTO) has developed a list of factors that would define state trading. A state organization that is involved in one or many of the activities listed in Table 1 may be defined as a state trader.

The definition of a state trader as expressed by GATT is open to interpretation. Whereas the list of characteristics of state traders covers a broad base of operations, there is evidence that an STE must affect the quantity or direction of the commodity traded. For an STE's actions to be of concern to other trading nations, that STE must be distorting trade,

Table 1: Characteristics of State Traders: GATT

(a)	purchase of all, or a significant percentage of, domestic production
(b)	intervention purchases and sales (based on predetermined floor and ceiling prices)
(c)	involvement in support schemes for domestic production
(d)	administration of marketing arrangements
(e)	import operations (possible monopoly on imports)
(f)	export operations (possible monopoly on exports)
(g)	domestic distribution of national production (possible monopoly)
(h)	domestic distribution of imports (possible monopoly)
(i)	quality control of domestic production (for export)
(j)	storage, shipping, handling, processing, packaging, insuring (and other export-related activities)
(k)	credit guarantees (or other assistance) for producers and processors
(l)	marketing activities (promotion activities for both exports and national consumption)
(m)	maintenance of emergency stocks (national defense preparedness or implementation of food security programs)
(n)	granting of licenses (for import, export, or production)
(o)	negotiation of long-term bilateral contracts for exports
(p)	implementation of quantitative restrictions (on imports/exports)
(q)	implementation of bilateral aid agreements

Source: "Notified Operations of State Trading Enterprises." WTO Secretariat's Report (1995), 15.

which implies it must be affecting quantity. Specifically, it must be altering the quantity imported or exported from the competitive equilibrium. If a state trader is affecting trade, it is assumed that it is doing so in accordance with some policy objective. The view of the policy objective versus the view of the effects will, at times, differ, which can lead to a divergence between perception and reality of STEs.

The theory of state trading has not been well developed in the economics literature. Most often, a model of imperfect competition is used if the state trader has monopoly power (exporter) or monopsony power (importer). State traders may have other characteristics that distinguish them from an open market, such as price pooling, export subsidies, or being government-owned cooperatives.

Consider Figure 1, where we have an excess demand for some commodity—for example, Canadian wheat (ED)—and an excess supply for Canadian wheat (ES); the world price is P_w and Q_w is the quantity traded.

Figure 1: Excess Supply and Demand for Canadian Wheat

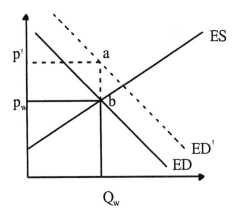

The competitive margin (basis)—that is, cost of doing business—is rectangle $P_w P'ab$, which is divided between private and state traders. The excess demand curve ED' is the excess demand after accounting for the basis. If the margin is larger under state trading, this basis would be a tax on producers or consumers, depending on which side of the market the STE operates, but would not affect the quantity traded. The principal trade issue in question is whether the existence of a state trader alters the level of Q_w from its competitive position. In Figure 1 the existence of state traders does not alter the volume; rather, it determines the magnitude of the margin. However, a government policy that subsidizes supply or shifts the demand will affect the quantity traded. Thus, it is the policy variables that are in play that matter, not the existence of an STE.

Suppose now that an exporting state trading enterprise has market power in the wheat market. The maximum profit will be where the marginal cost of exporting is equal to the marginal return in each market. In such a case, the exporter is practicing price discrimination and, accordingly, the level of trade will be altered from the competitive solution. This activity is consistent with the GATT, provided it is for commercial reasons and not political reasons. A similar result could be arrived at for a monopsony.

In terms of the earlier definitions of an STE, it is the policies carried out that can distort the markets and create unfair trade. We need to examine each STE separately to see how it operates and if it is being used as a policy instrument for the government. This would be consistent with the definitions given by GATT. Special attention needs to be paid to the export subsidies that would shift the excess supply curve to the right, and the tariff and nontariff barriers that would shift the excess demand curve to the left. Any shift of the curves in the opposite direction would aid trading partners and be of no concern. A reduction in supply or an increase in demand would lead to higher prices and more trade, which would benefit other exporters.

Alston and Gray (1997) have shown that similar results regarding prices, volumes, and revenues can be achieved either by a state trader like the CWB or by the export enhancement program (EEP) in the U.S. The Commodity Credit Corporation (CCC) is, therefore, a form of STE, set up to implement government policy. There are, however, significant differences between the CWB and the CCC in that the CWB does not carry out government policy, while the CCC is a policy instrument of the United States Department of Agriculture (USDA). This distinction is important in that the CWB does distort trade—that is, it price discriminates—from the competitive solution so as to maximize producer returns (Kraft, Furtan, and Tyrchniewicz 1996) but does not do so at the discretion of Agriculture Canada.[2] The CCC and use of EEP on the other hand is a direct policy instrument of the USDA to achieve higher market share for U.S. wheat farmers. The perception and the reality of organizations such as the CCC often differ, because it is the impact of the organization's mandate and operations which matters, not its legislative structure.

In this next section we provide a brief description of the two STEs used in the grain trade in the U.S. and Canada. Both of these organizations are functions of government policy and fall within the definition of STEs given earlier in the paper.[3]

In the United States, the Commodity Credit Corporation was formed in 1933 in the first Agricultural Adjustment Act in order to deal with the effects of the Depression. It was "created to stabilize, support and protect farm income and prices; to maintain balanced and adequate supplies of agricultural commodities, including products, foods, feeds and fibers; and to help in the orderly distribution of these commodities" (Canada-U.S. Joint Commission on Grains 1995, 51). The CCC is owned and operated by the U.S. government. It does not have staff—all of its operations are carried out by other U.S. government departments such as the consolidated Farm Service Agency, the Foreign Agricultural Service, and others (Canada-U.S. Joint Commission on Grains 1995). There is a USDA board of directors under the direction of the Secretary of Agriculture. The CCC is authorized to finance a number of support and export programs through the use of its capital stock of $100 million, bolstered by the ability to borrow up to $30 billion at any time. One of the roles the CCC played in the past was to support the U.S. wheat price through the purchase of grain from producers, removing it from the market. Because the U.S. is such a large producer, this resulted in U.S. support of the world wheat price and the CCC's acquisition of large stocks of wheat. In May 1985, the Export Enhancement Program (EEP) was introduced, in part to help dispose of those stocks. Initially, the EEP program came in the form of bonus wheat from the CCC stocks. This changed in 1992 after CCC stocks had fallen, and the EEP bonuses were in the form of cash incentives (Simonot 1997).

The Foreign Agricultural Service (FAS) sets minimum prices and maximum bonuses for commodities sold under the program. Exporters compete for sales. They negotiate a sales price with an exporter, determine the needed export bonus, and submit that to the FAS as a bid. Bids are not public but must fall within the minimums and maximums described above. The idea is that the competition for EEP dollars will keep the bonuses at a minimum. There were four criteria set for the EEP at its inception: first, it should result in a net increase of U.S. exports; second, sales should be targeted at competitors which subsidize their exports; third, it should provide a net benefit to the U.S. economy; and, fourth, it should be budget neutral (Gardner 1996). Originally, most EEP sales were to North African and Middle Eastern markets (Algeria, Egypt, Morocco, Tunisia, and Yemen) and to the Philippines. In 1987, EEP was expanded and included China and the Soviet Union. In 1989 the guidelines were changed to have the EEP: counter competitors' subsidies and advance Uruguay Round negotiations; develop, expand, or maintain U.S. markets; consider the implications of EEP sales on nonsubsidizing export countries; and ensure that bonuses would be the minimum necessary to achieve the program's export expansion and trade policy objectives.

The 1990 farm bill mandated that a minimum of $500 million per year be used to implement the EEP program until 1995. "In addition, the 1990 Budget Reconciliation Act required an extra $1 billion in export programs (which include the EEP) for the period from October 1993 until September 1995 if the United States failed to enter into an agreement under the Uruguay Round of the GATT by the end of June 1992. This legislation is termed as the 'GATT trigger'" (Canada-U.S. Joint Commission on Grains 1995, 55).

The CCC acts as a state trader in part through the use of the EEP. The purpose of the EEP was to increase U.S. market share, thus increase Q_w. Using the model illustrated in Figure 1, one could model the theoretical impact of an export subsidy such as the EEP. Export subsidies are generally seen to move the excess supply curve of the exporting country to the right. This has the effect of driving down the world price and, usually, increasing the quantity exported. As the EEP has been targeted to specific markets, there is question as to whether it actually increased the quantity the U.S. exported. In fact, there is mounting evidence that the EEP did not meet its first objective: to increase U.S. market share (GAO 1997). There is, however, little doubt that it decreased the price in those markets. This led other exporters to vacate EEP markets in favor of markets where prices were not depressed.

The Canadian Wheat Board (CWB) is the sole exporter of western Canadian wheat and barley. It also sells all western Canadian wheat and barley for human consumption within Canada. The CWB was created in 1935 (after a brief existence following World War One) and received its monopoly in 1943 through an act of Parliament: *The Canadian Wheat Board Act*. The federal government does not directly finance the operations of the CWB, but does guarantee its borrowings. It also helps finance sales credit. The Credit Grains Sales Program (CGSP) offers credit for the purchase of wheat and barley to importing STEs. This program covers approximately 5 to 10 percent of CWB sales (Canada-U.S. Joint Commission on Grains 1995). There are other credit programs offered by the Canadian government, but they are not exclusive to the CWB.

The prices the CWB receives for grain are pooled by type and grade over the crop year; thus, every farmer receives the same price (less the basis) for the same quality grain. Western Canadian grain farmers receive an initial payment, guaranteed by the federal government, of about 80 percent of the projected returns for the year. In 1986 the government paid over $200 million into the wheat pool account to remove a deficit created because the initial payment farmers received was higher than the CWB could get from the market (the CWB has made payments into the wheat and barley pool in other years as well). This initial payment guarantee has an implied value even if the government does not make a pay-out in any given year.

In 1993-94, the CWB moved to a contract system for timing the sourcing of grain from producers. Producers sign a contract for a certain quantity and grade of grain, to be delivered before a specific date. There are four delivery deadlines in the year. Within a few weeks after the last date to sign a specific contract, the CWB calculates the percentage of the contracted grain needed and calls it forward (CWB 1994). Through its sales program, the CWB attempts to extract the best price possible from each market. The CWB analyzes the demand curve in each market and prices accordingly. This price discrimination is possible only if Canadian grain is viewed differently than grain from other countries and if there is no arbitrage of CWB grain between markets. Price discrimination is also possible only if there is but one seller, or a few sellers acting collusively.

The operations of the CWB are often questioned by the U.S. The CWB can make forward contracts and be certain it can source the grain, because it knows what supplies are available on Canadian farms as well as being the single exporter. Millers in the U.S. may wish to lock in some of their supplies from the CWB rather than buy on the spot market in the U.S. This is equivalent to the CWB having a long open position with no corresponding price risk. Firms in a competitive market would never be able to carry such risk. It is possible that the CWB could dump grain into the U.S. market at below world prices and average the returns with other sales, thus hiding the action through the pooled price, but such moves by the CWB would be actionable under the new rules of the WTO.[4]

Magnitude of State Trading in Wheat[5]

Overall, since the mid-century, state trading by exporters has increased substantially, while state trading on the importing side peaked during the 1980s and has since declined. To illustrate the significance of state trading in the world wheat market, and the role played by the U.S. and Canada, Table 2, created by McCalla and Schmitz (1982) has been reproduced and updated. There have been a number of significant structural changes in the wheat trade over the past two decades. In the late 1980s, several Central and South American countries privatized their state traders. This change was led by Brazil, the major importer of the region. Argentina also privatized its major grain exporter. During this same time, the USSR itself disappeared, taking its state importer out of the market. By contrast, in 1985 the U.S. introduced the EEP in response to the EU's (at that time, the EEC's) increasing use of export subsidies by becoming state traders in wheat. "With the introduction of the EEP and the EU Export Restitution payments, both the United States (U.S.) and the European Union became major state traders" (Schmitz 1996, 13). This meant that all major grain exporters were now state traders, with the exception of Argentina.

The two recent periods added in Table 2 have been calculated with the U.S. included as a state exporter of wheat and with the U.S. counted as a private trader. It is clear that both the CCC and the EEP are manifestations of state exporting; however, not all U.S. exports pass through

Table 2: State Trading in Wheat—Percentage of Volume of Principal Exporters Accounted for by State Traders

				U.S. included as a state trader		U.S. not included as a state trader	
	1953-57	1963-67	1973-77	1983-87	1990-94	1983-87	1990-94
	percent	percent	percent	percent	percent	percent	percent
1. Private exporters to private importers	10.7	5.9	4.4	0.9	4.3	1.2	9.4
2. Private exporters to state importers	33.3	51.2	56.6	43.4	2.0	54.6	34.1
3. State exporters to private importers	28.3	8.1	4.3	2.2	12.1	1.9	7.0
4. State exporters to state importers	27.7	34.8	34.7	53.5	81.6	42.3	49.5
Summary Exports by private traders (1+2)	44.0	57.1	61.0	44.3	6.3	55.8	43.5
Exports by state traders (3+4)	56.0	42.9	39.0	55.7	93.7	44.2	56.5
Imports by private traders (1+3)	39.0	14.0	8.7	3.1	16.4	3.1	16.4
Imports by state traders (2+4)	61.0	86.0	91.3	96.9	83.6	96.9	83.6
Volume of trade included above (000 m.t.)	23,475	49,891	60,385	88,514	90,021	88,514	90,021
Total world exports (000 m.t.)	25,596	56,397	63,506	94,064	97,742	94,064	97,742

Sources: McCalla and Schmitz 1982, 64.
　　　　1983-87—International Wheat Council, World Wheat Statistics, 1984-87 issues.
　　　　1990-94—International Wheat Council, World Grain Statistics, 1991-94 issues.
　　　　(Updated by Simonot 1997).

these channels every year, so not all transactions are affected directly. Thus, the U.S. exercises state trading, but not on 100 percent of exports all the time. Due to its significance in the wheat market, the U.S. can often exert substantial influence by periodically affecting trade on a large portion of its exports. The true measure of state trading taking the range of U.S. actions falls between the two extremes presented in Table 2.

Interactions between Major State Traders

Table 2 indicates that sales from state trader to state trader have increased from approximately 35 percent in 1973-77 to between 50 and 82 percent in the 1990s. These interactions have the potential to result in the interesting bilateral monopoly negotiation problem where both sides try to exert their market power to obtain favorable sales agreements. Kostecki (1982) gives an example of this by implementing a strategy of using stocks and state trading to generate market instability. The idea is to give the impression of a shortage by understating stock or production levels and indicating that import requirements would be high. This encourages exporters to maintain production at a high level, thus providing ample, cheap supplies when final import demands are less than forecast. This strategy was attributed to the USSR in past years.

Table 3 illustrates the significance of the major traders in the wheat market. Average market shares for importers and exporters have been calculated for ten-year periods beginning in 1950. The table shows the relative importance of various countries and how some shifting has occurred over this period. The most notable changes are the massive increase in EU exports throughout the period and the decline in exports from the former Soviet Union (FSU). Over the period, the EU moved from being the largest net importer to being the third largest net exporter. The changes in composition of the EU over this period are not fully captured in Table 3. The United Kingdom, a significant importer, was not included in the EU until very recently, so the majority of EU exports came from France. The FSU shifted from net exporter in the 1950s to the largest net importer, then dropped out of the market almost entirely by the mid-1990s, due to severe restructuring difficulties. It is clear that there are only a handful of major exporters. Imports are more dispersed, but a few countries took substantial shares at various times through the period (Simonot 1997).

Table 3: Average Wheat Market Shares for the Major Importing and
         Exporting Nations

	1950-59	1960-69	1970-79	1980-89	1990-94
	percent	percent	percent	percent	percent
Exporters					
Canada	29.1	22.0	20.2	19.2	21.5
U.S.	39.2	38.0	43.5	38.7	33.9
Australia	9.7	12.4	13.3	12.8	10.8
Argentina	8.7	6.1	4.4	5.9	5.7
EU	6.1	9.2	9.2	16.2	20.1
FSU	4.2	8.1	4.5	0.3	-
Turkey	0.6	-	0.6	0.6	2.6
Total Exports (million tonnes)	27.2	50.5	65.9	96.1	98.8
Percent of total trade included	97.6	95.8	95.7	93.7	94.6
Importers					
EU	18.7	9.6	7.8	3.1	1.4
Japan	7.8	7.2	8.3	5.9	5.9
China	-	9.1	8.2	12.2	9.3
FSU	0.4	5.2	9.8	19.5	15.6
Turkey	0.6	0.9	0.3	-	-
India	7.8	9.6	3.8	1.2	0.8
Total Imports (million tonnes)	27.2	50.5	65.9	96.1	98.8
Percent of total trade included	35.3	41.6	38.2	41.9	33.0

Sources: 1950-59—UNFAO, World Grain Trade Statistics.
         1960-79—International Wheat Council, Review of the World Wheat Situation.
         1980-89—International Wheat Council, World Wheat Statistics.
         1990-94—International Wheat Council, World Grain Statistics.

Chronology of the Canada-U.S. Wheat Dispute[6]

Trade in wheat between Canada and the U.S. has existed for all
of the twentieth century. Two periods that stand out are during World
War Two, when Canada exported wheat into the U.S. because of large

surpluses and, more recently, the period of the EEP. The EEP raised internal U.S. grain prices while lowering the world price. This made the U.S. market more attractive for the CWB.

Figure 2: Canadian Wheat Exports to U.S., 1919-1997

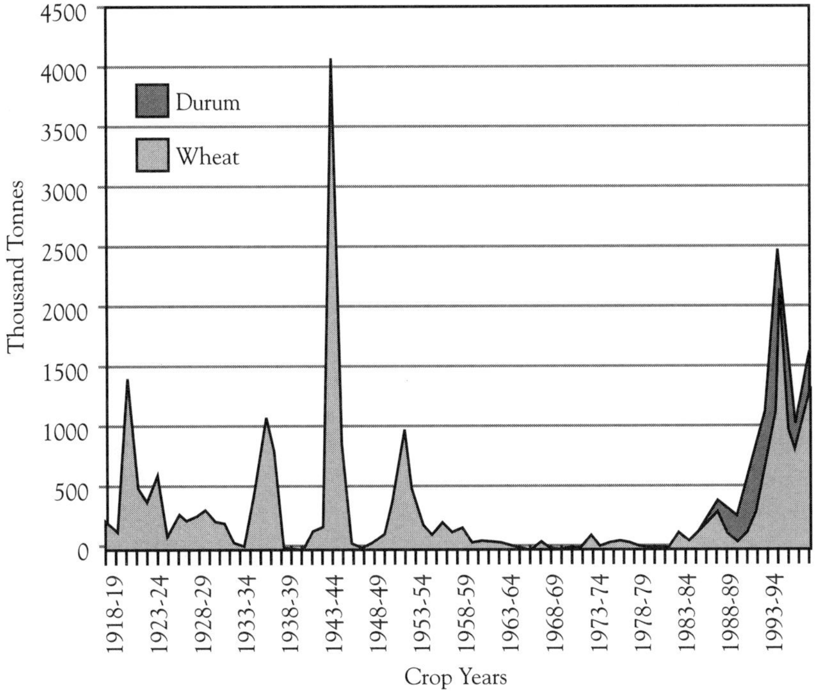

Sources: 1918-55—Board of Grain Commissioners Report, Trade and Commerce.
1955-72—Canadian Grain Commission, Canadian Grain Exports.
1972-96—Canadian Grain Commission, Grain Statistics Handbook.

As can be seen in Figure 2, the most dramatic increase since World War Two came during the 1993-94 crop year, when floods devastated grain farmers in the United States, creating large shortages of feed wheat—wheat intended for animal rather than human consumption. Supply was so limited in the U.S. that American millers blended some of the Canadian feed wheat with higher quality wheat to produce wheat flour, some of which was exported under U.S. export subsidies, angering many American farmers. High quality Canadian wheat exports—particularly

durum wheat, which is used for making pasta—also continued to
expand, but it was lower quality feed wheat exports that grew most
rapidly. Even before the flood, American wheat growers were
complaining that Canadian wheat was undercutting the price of domestic wheat, and pointed to Canadian government transportation
subsidies (through the Western Grain Transportation Act) as the
culprit. For their part, the American grain multinationals complained
about unfairly subsidized Canadian Wheat Board exports going to
third markets such as Mexico.

By May of 1993, Agriculture Secretary Mike Espy and U.S. Trade
Representative Mickey Kantor were asked by midwestern and northern
tier congressmen and senators to consider subsidizing American wheat
exports to Mexico under the EEP, in order to compete with, and displace,
Canadian exports. Within weeks, Espy announced that EEP would, indeed, be used to help American wheat exports to Mexico. The Canadian
minister at the Geneva mission, Pierre Gosselin, accused the United States
of using the EEP to squeeze Canada out of Mexico, a traditional market
for Canadian wheat. According to Gosselin, this was the first time that
the EEP, originally created to counter European Community agricultural
export subsidies, was used directly against Canada in a third market in
which the United States and Canada constituted the only competitors.
The Canadian government alleged that U.S. actions violated Article
701(4) of the Canada-U.S. Free Trade Agreement (CUSTA), which required each country to "take into account the export interests of the other
Party in the use of any export subsidy on any agricultural good exported
to third countries" such as Mexico, if these subsidies have a "prejudicial"
effect on the export interests of the other country. In return, the U.S.
government argued that Article 701(4), while a laudable statement of
principle, was effectively unenforceable (*Financial Post* 1993).

The wheat dispute intensified when, at the request of the president,
the U.S. International Trade Commission (ITC) launched an investigation into Canadian durum wheat exports on 18 January 1994. Clinton
made his request under Section 22 of the 1933 Agricultural Adjustment
Act, under which the ITC was asked to investigate whether Canadian
durum wheat was being imported "under such conditions or in such quantities as to render or to tend to render ineffective, or materially interfere
with, the price support, payment and production adjustment program
conducted by the department of agriculture for wheat" (Winnipeg *Free
Press* 1994).

Although Canadian Minister of Agriculture and Agri-Food, Ralph Goodale, claimed that he was "not spooked" by Washington's action—it could, after all, be discontinued at any time—the wheat investigation had clearly lifted the profile of the wheat dispute and pushed the Canadian government to resolve that specific disagreement in order to take the pressure off other agricultural trade concerns, including the supply management sector. In particular, the United States wanted Canada to submit to a voluntary export restraint agreement, limiting wheat exports to the United States for a period of years.

Although negotiations continued among officials, little progress was made. Senator Richard Lugar and Congressman Pat Roberts, both of whom were chairs of the Committee on Agriculture, were pushing for increased price disclosure from the Canadian Wheat Board. Since the Wheat Board was a state "monopoly" trading agency they, along with other House and Senate members, felt that it should be under a higher standard of disclosure than the private grain companies. The Canadians, on the other hand, took heart in an independent audit completed in early March by a company agreed to by both countries, in which, of the 105 Canadian Wheat Board export contracts examined, covering a period from January 1989 to July 1992, there were only three cases of subsidies in early 1989. Moreover, the U.S. was about to sign the new GATT agreement, giving up its rights under Section 22 of the Agricultural Adjustment Act.[7]

By the end of April, the dispute had entered its most acrimonious phase, as both sides carried their campaign to third countries. The Canadian Minister of Agriculture traveled to China and Korea, where EEP-subsidized wheat sales had recently reduced Canada's market share. Meanwhile, claiming that both the United States and Argentina had lost market share in Brazil to subsidized Canadian wheat, Espy convinced the Argentines to demand that the Canadians explain their pricing policies (*Financial Post* 1994).

By this time, Canada's International Trade Minister Roy MacLaren had reluctantly come to the conclusion that the U.S. government fully intended to carry out its threat of unilaterally imposing a quota on Canadian wheat imports, and that it was better to negotiate a higher cap than to allow a lower cap to be imposed. After months of arguing the contrary— that his government would never agree to such a settlement—he felt that a voluntary export restraint was now in Canada's interests as long as he could keep the U.S. from unilaterally imposing quotas or countervailing duties on Canadian grain.

The Canada-U.S. Wheat Deal of 1 August 1994

On 1 August, a three-part agreement was reached, which both sides felt was politically acceptable (Agriculture Canada 1994). It held, first, that Canada was subjected to two separate caps: if durum wheat exports were between 300,000 and 450,000 tonnes they would face a tariff of $23 per tonne, and any amount above 450,000 tonnes would encounter a prohibitive tariff (or cap); Canadian Wheat Board wheat (wheat from the western provinces only) would be capped at 1,050,000 million tonnes. Second, a "Blue Ribbon" Committee comprised of six to ten private-sector members of the two countries would be established in order to determine the impact of grain marketing institutions and programs in each country on bilateral and third-country trade, with a final report to be delivered by 1 July 1995. And, third, a one-year "peace clause" would prevent the United States from launching any further trade actions, and Canada from challenging any U.S. actions under either the NAFTA or the GATT, until 1 July 1995.

Both governments claimed satisfaction with the agreement. The U.S. government felt that the cap was low enough to protect U.S. producers from a flood of Canadian wheat imports for the current crop year. In addition, the committee ensured that the practices of the Canadian Wheat Board would come under intense scrutiny, and the findings of the committee would give the U.S. government political ammunition to pressure the Canadians to change their marketing practices. The Canadian government came to the opposite conclusion. It felt that the cap was high enough that it would not overly impede Canadian wheat exports to the United States, and that its own members on the committee would be able to protect the integrity of the Canadian Wheat Board, while exposing the subsidies and unfair practices employed in the U.S. grain-handling system.

At least initially, a majority of farm groups in both countries were unhappy with the agreement negotiated by their respective governments. U.S. grain growers felt that the cap was too high and that the agreement should have been extended to barley imports as well. Many Canadian wheat growers felt that their government had set a dangerous precedent by agreeing to the cap, and some felt that the cap was definitely below Canada's potential wheat exports to the United States. In other words, Canadian exports would be artificially capped at a low level through the voluntary export restraint, and Canadians might be forced to negotiate future export caps after the one-year agreement lapsed.

Many factors that produced the dispute then are as evident today as they were in 1993 and 1994. Both countries continue to support agriculture through a variety of government programs. While very little has changed in this regard, Canada has removed the freight subsidy on the export of grains from Western Canada as a result of past GATT negotiations and budgetary concerns. The removal of the freight subsidy in effect lowered the farm gate price of grain on the Canadian prairies and encouraged farmers to look for markets closer to home. One such market is the domestic U.S. market, which can be reached at a much lower cost than export markets overseas. It may be concluded, then, that the U.S. insistence that this subsidy be removed has increased, not decreased, the incentive for Canadian grain to move south. If the CWB export monopoly were removed, farmers and other exporters would likely move more grain into the U.S. market. The CWB restricts exports to the U.S. to keep the peace with the U.S. grain industry. Again, if northern U.S. grain farmers get their way and have the CWB monopoly removed, they may get a perverse result.

Perceptions[8]

The perceptions of the wheat dispute and the STEs involved have not always coincided with reality. As well as disagreements between the two nations, there is not consensus within the countries of the cause and effect of the wheat trade. We now turn to the perceptions of both Canadian and U.S. government and industry regarding STEs and the wheat dispute. The 1993-94 wheat dispute focused attention on Canada and the U.S. state traders in grain. Both institutions were hailed as culprits that increased the import of Canadian grain into the U.S. Many in the U.S. raised concerns that the CWB was acting as an unfair trader, subsidizing its exports either to the U.S. or abroad, and driving down the price received by U.S. farmers. Many Canadians argued that it was the U.S. EEP that was driving down international prices, and the flow of Canadian grain into the U.S. was merely market arbitrage.

Canadian Perceptions

It is evident from the above chronology that the EEP has been used as a specific policy tool. This is illustrated by the use of EEP to subsidize U.S. wheat exports into Mexico at the request of U.S. congressmen from the wheat belt. There are other instances in which the EEP was targeted at countries where the major traders were not subsidizing their exports. The CWB raised the concern about EEP being used to target Canadian sales thus:

> Examples of markets where the U.S. has failed to consider Canada's interests [in the use of the EEP], despite the fact the EU is not a major player, include the Philippines, Brazil, Columbia, Mexico and Venezuela.... Allocations of EEP to both Finland (135,000 tonnes) and Norway (160,000 tonnes) on June 24, 1993, also appeared to be directed at non-EU competitors.... Canada is a major player in both of these markets and the EEP allocations displaced imports of high-quality Canadian wheat.

A number of Canadian farm groups, as well as the CWB, argued that the EEP was a large factor in the grain dispute. For example, from the National Farmers Union (Canada):

> We recall with considerable clarity the outcry from the U.S. producers over imports of Canadian durum during the 1993-94 crop year. Although world durum stocks were extremely tight, the U.S. continued to subsidize durum exports. The USDA projected durum production to be 2.1 million tonnes, while domestic consumption was forecasted to be 2.42 million tonnes. Despite this tight domestic situation, USDA's export program targeted to move 816 thousand tonnes of durum to offshore markets, mostly with EEP subsidies.

Some argued that the EEP had the effect of raising the U.S. domestic grain price, making it a more attractive market for Canadian grain. Two examples:

Canadian Wheat Board Advisory Committee:

> As long as the U.S. continues to use the EEP to subsidize sales into third country markets, Canadian grain will be attracted into the U.S. to meet customer demand and achieve the best possible prices for farmers.

Prairie Pools:

> There is absolutely no question that the existence of the EEP serves to make the U.S. an attractive market for Canadian grain (especially wheat and durum) producers. It does so in two ways: by removing

grain from the domestic market it maintains U.S. domestic prices at higher levels than would otherwise exist; and it reduces prices in targeted offshore markets, thus reducing the return to Canadian farmers on sales to these markets.

Others disagree that the EEP acted as a driving force in increasing Canada's grain exports to the U.S., among them the Alberta Barley Commission:

> EEP has had little effect on the gap between the two country prices. Thus EEP has had little effect on the incentive to sell Canadian barley into the U.S. market…. However EEP has distorted the relative returns between CWB prices and the domestic market.

Some Canadian groups have compared the EEP to Canada's rail freight subsidy for grain under the Western Grain Transportation Act (WGTA). For example, the Western Canadian Wheat Growers Association (WCWGA):

> Given that Canada is proceeding with plans to convert the WGTA subsidy to a direct income support program, we consider it imperative that the U.S. government take similar measures to convert EEP… the export assistance paid by each government, [through EEP and the WGTA] on a production basis, is not dissimilar.

and Dominion Malting:

> The "crow benefit" [WGTA subsidy] versus EEP incentives is an issue which likely should be considered in terms of how the two countries compete against each other in export markets.

However, The Canadian Wheat Board Advisory Committee disagrees:

> Western Grain Transportation Act (WGTA) payments have absolutely no effect on the export price of Canadian wheat and barley in the U.S. or off-shore markets.

United States Perceptions

Although a number of U.S. farm groups raised concerns about Canada's WGTA, it is also evident that the U.S. believes that the Canadian Wheat Board may be subsidizing wheat exports into the U.S. The USDA is publicizing the fact that Canadian wheat exports to the U.S. are 32 percent over the 1994 cap levels (red spring exports to the U.S. are 35 percent over, and durum exports 21 percent over the wheat deal cap). American pressure is mounting to get the Canadian wheat exports down to the 1994 levels (*Western Producer* 1997). Producers and producer groups have voiced concern that the Canadian Wheat Board is exporting wheat and barley into the United States and undercutting their price.

BRA submission—Ronald Selzler:

> Through their wheat board pricing practice, they [Canada] have the ability to dump in our market.

This is a sentiment repeated by the USDA:

> U.S. producers, for instance, have complained that the Canadian Wheat Board (CWB) subsidizes grain through its pricing policies to their competitive disadvantage. (Economic Research Service [ERS] 1996, 5)

and by North Dakota Senator Kent Conrad:

> Many analysts believe that the CWB's pricing practices differ from that of a perfectly competitive firm and that its prices in the U.S. tend to undercut U.S. prices.

The Canadian Wheat Board's price nontransparency and price pooling are often cited as means by which the CWB can subsidize exports. The American Farm Bureau Federation asserts that:

> There is another issue that involves price transparency, or the lack of price transparency with respect to the way the Canadian Wheat Board (CWB) operates. The CWB can net $20 to $25 per ton more by selling wheat in the United States than they can by selling it into the depressed world market. The lack of pricing transparency allows the CWB to have standing price orders that are slightly below U.S. offers.

and the U.S. General Accounting Office states that:

> U.S. critics of CWB contend that CWB has an unfair pricing advantage due to its status as the single-desk selling authority. According to one USDA official, the day-to-day replacement cost for wheat is more readily apparent in the United States with its commodity markets than is true of CWB. (GAO 1996, 45)

This view of the CWB as a means to subsidize exports persists with the linking of the CWB to the EEP. Sharold Geist, Chairman, North Dakota Wheat Commission says:

> The Canadian Wheat Board continues to be critical of EEP while clinging to a different brand of price discrimination that the CWB has practiced worldwide for decades. EEP was introduced in the late 1980s in response to these, and other unfair trading practices, that existed in the world market at the time.

and, from Commissioner of the North Dakota Department of Agriculture, Sarah Vogel:

> The U.S. Export Enhancement Program (EEP) should be examined as should the Canadian Wheat Board's (CWB's) price differentials for various markets which effectively match the U.S. EEP. These methods both move grain and maintain markets, but do not obtain maximum prices from buyers.

As noted in the comments by Sarah Vogel, the crux of many of the arguments about the CWB acting as an export subsidy would imply that the CWB is not maximizing Canadian producer returns. From the U.S. General Accounting Office:

> Some U.S. officials are also concerned about CWB undercutting U.S. producers using its grain quality standards. According to USDA officials, CWB has used high quality as a marketing strategy, often providing higher protein content in its wheat than the customer requests and thus developing an expectation that CWB's wheat is a better value for the money. (GAO 1996, 45)

In addition, the USDA explicitly sees the Canadian Wheat Board as a policy tool:

> Prices of commodities in question are most often fixed directly by the STE or by the Government through parastatal organizations.... Because price stability is an integral part of the domestic policy agenda of most developed nations, many parastatal organizations also participate in intervention activities. Hence, management and disposal of stocks is a common feature of these enterprises and government-set targets for reserve stocks are maintained and managed—often exclusively—by state trading enterprises. Activities of the Canadian Wheat Board (CWB) among exporters, and the Japanese Food Agency (JFA), among

importers, would be the best illustrations of developed country state trading enterprises being used as instruments to attain domestic policy objectives. (Economic Research Service 1996, 6)

Perception of the effects of a state trader vary dramatically with what one sees as the alternative. From the American Farm Bureau Federation:

Obviously there is a difference of opinion of the fairness or equability of the CWB and the way it markets wheat versus the free market system used in the United States.

and from the GAO:

Grain traders in the United States are "price takers," or are required to buy their grain at the given market price without being able to affect that price. The CWB's exclusive purchasing authority over wheat and barley for human consumption provides CWB with a more secure source of supply, as well as more control, than would be the case for a private exporter. (GAO 1996, 45)

and the USDA:

Consequently [due to price pooling] STEs have greater flexibility in discretionary pricing in the international market (through delayed payments to domestic producers), an arrangement not available to private exporters who have to compete with other domestic sellers in acquiring exportable products. It is also suggested that STEs that control domestic supplies or exports have little uncertainty in sourcing supplies. (ERS 1996, 8)

Yet the USDA also notes:

Commercial exporters like Cargill can source from various countries to fulfill their sales commitments, a benefit that is normally unavailable to STEs. (ERS 1996, 8)

These comments contrast with others which argue that the alternative to the Canadian Wheat Board is not perfect competition. For example, from Norm Sullivan, President, Montana Farmers Union:

Growing pressure from commodity groups to pry marketing authority from the non-profit Canadian Wheat Board would only divide the united marketing front of Canadian farmers and place them at the mercy of the profit-driven multinational corporations.

It is clear from these quotations that there is a perception in the U.S. that the CWB regularly subsidizes Canadian wheat farmers and thus distorts wheat trade. The reality is that the CWB seeks to maximize returns to Canadian producers through price discrimination; it does not subsidize wheat producers except in years where the pool account is negative. Canadians perceive that the EEP has largely been responsible for Canadian grain moving into the U.S. domestic market. The reality is that the EEP did impact the trade flows in the late 1980s and early 1990s, but current grain movement has to do with the removal of the Canadian freight rate subsidies. Thus the perception and the realities do not always coincide.

Conclusions

Many countries use STEs in agriculture and in the grain trade in particular. Certainly the CWB in Canada and the CCC in the U.S. are examples. For an STE's actions to be of concern to other trading nations, that STE must be distorting trade, which implies it must be moving the quantity imported or exported from the competitive equilibrium. State traders can distort trade through activities such as price discrimination or through subsidizing/taxing exports and imports. In the first case, the STE is maximizing revenue without government transfers (basically following standard business practice). In the second case the STE is carrying out government policies with tax dollars. Thus, it is the policy variables that are in play that matter (for example any domestic policy that subsidizes production of a traded commodity will distort trade). Accordingly, we have argued that it is not so much the presence of STEs that distorts trade, but rather the domestic policies of countries that tax or subsidize exports/imports that are the problems.

Although the specific meteorological circumstances that led to the 1993 wheat dispute have passed, there is still tension surrounding the Canada-U.S. grain trade. The U.S. is currently not using the EEP and, thus, the CCC is no longer operating as an STE. Canada has removed export subsidies, such as the WGTA, which has led to an increased flow of grain into the U.S. market. This is once again eliciting mounting pressure from U.S. legislators and grain producers to stem the Canada-U.S. grain trade, with specific concern focused on Canada's state trader in grain. Using the arguments about lack of transparency and concern about the CWB undercutting U.S. wheat exports, U.S. trade representatives are giving notice that the U.S. plans to target STEs at the next round of GATT (*Western Producer* 1997).

The CWB has been investigated by various arms of the U.S. government and found to be operating within the law and spirit of fair trade. This, however, has not lessened the criticism by many U.S. producer groups and the USDA. The CWB's export monopoly does remain a trade irritant, however its removal would expand the volume of Canadian grain entering the U.S. market, not reduce it. This last condition reinforces the difference between the perception and reality of STEs and the Canada-U.S. grain trade.

NOTES

1. The General Agreement on Tariffs and Trade (GATT) was the source of international trade rules prior to 1994. At that point, an institution, the World Trade Organization (WTO) was formed in order to be the arbitrator of international trade rules agreed to in the Uruguay Round of the GATT negotiations; the GATT rules are now embedded within the WTO. These terms are used interchangeably in this paper.

2. There are exceptions. The voluntary export restraint of durum agreed to by the Canadian government in 1994-95 did require the CWB to restrict exports to the U.S.

3. There are two examples of state trading outside of agriculture that illustrate some interesting economic conditions. The first of these is the former Potash Corporation of Saskatchewan, which was fully privatized in 1989-90. The second is Hydro Quebec, which is a crown corporation wholly owned by the Quebec provincial government.

The PCS was a major exporter of potash to the U.S. In 1984, the U.S. government brought dumping charges against the PCS because the STE was selling into the U.S. market below the cost of production (Picketts, Schmitz, and Schmitz 1991). The reason PCS was able to follow this policy was because it was wholly owned by the Saskatchewan government. Why did PCS follow this strategy? The potash market was very soft and the Saskatchewan government wished to mobilize employment in the potash mines. This led to overproduction and, ultimately, to dumping once stocks became too large. It was clear that this state trader was carrying out government policy.

Hydro Quebec regularly exports power into the U.S. market and is a state trader. In the case of Hydro Quebec, it prices its electricity at rates similar to those in the U.S. Again the perception and reality of STEs' business practices and policy decisions need to be carefully examined.

4. There is question as to whether the CWB increases or decreases the Q_w traded. If the CWB earns premiums from high-priced markets, as demonstrated by Kraft, Furtan, and Tyrchniewicz (1996), this added revenue is reflected in a higher pooled price

received by farmers. This would encourage producers to produce more grain, which then gets sold into markets with highly elastic demand (markets where increased quantity sold has little effect on the price). If the CWB adds cost to the basis, resulting in a lower farm-gate price for wheat and barley (Carter and Loyns 1996), then producers would have the incentive to produce and export less.

5. This section draws heavily on the work by David Simonot in "An Examination of International State Trading in Wheat." Unpublished M.Sc. thesis, University of Saskatchewan, Saskatoon, 1997.

6. This section is in large part from a paper by G.P Marchildon and W.H Furtan, "The 1993-94 Wheat War: Lessons for Canada-U.S. Relations?" n.d.

7. The GATT/World Trade Organization (WTO) agreement was actually signed by the U.S. government on 15 April 1994.

8. Unless otherwise noted, the quotes in this section come from submissions to the Canada-U.S. Joint Commission on Grains (1996).

REFERENCES

Agriculture Canada. 1994. *Backgrounder: Canada-U.S. Wheat Agreement.* Ottawa: Agriculture and Agri-Food Canada.

Alston, Julian, and Richard Gray. 1997. "North American Agricultural Trade Policies: Export Subsidies and State Trading." Paper presented at The Conference on World Agriculture, Ankara, Turkey, 18-20 September 1997.

Baban, Roy. 1977. "State Trading and the GATT." *Journal of World Trade Law* 11: 334-53.

Canada, Ministry of International Trade. 1993. *North American Free Trade Agreement.* Ottawa: Ministry of International Trade.

Canada, Ministry of Trade and Commerce. 1918-55. *Board of Grain Commissioners Report.* Ottawa: Ministry of Trade and Commerce.

Canada-United States Joint Commission on Grains. 1995. *Final Report.* William M. Miner and James Warren Miller, co-chairs. Winnipeg: Agriculture and Agri-Food Canada.

Canadian Grain Commission. 1955-72. *Canadian Grain Exports.* Winnipeg: Canadian Grain Commission.

_____. *Grain Statistics Handbook.* 1972-96. Winnipeg: Canadian Grain Commission.

Canadian Wheat Board. 1994. *Annual Report 1993-94.* Winnipeg: Canadian Wheat Board.

Carter, Colin A., and R.M.A. Loyns. 1996. *The Economics of Single Desk Selling of Western Canadian Grain.* Report to Alberta Agriculture. Edmonton: Alberta Agriculture.

Economic Research Service (ERS). 1996. *Economics of State Trading: A Concept Paper*. Preliminary Draft. Washington: ERS.

Financial Post. 1994. (17 May).

Gardner, Bruce L. 1996. "The Political Economy of the Export Enhancement Program for Wheat." In Anne O. Kruger, ed., *The Political Economy of Trade Protection*. Chicago: University of Chicago Press.

General Agreement on Tariffs and Trade. 1969. *Basic Instruments and Selected Documents, Volume IV—Text of the General Agreement*. Geneva: GATT.

International Wheat Council. 1960-79. *Review of the World Wheat Situation*. London: International Wheat Council.

_____. *World Grain Statistics*. 1991-94. London: International Wheat Council.

Lloyd, P.J. 1982. "State Trading and the Theory of International Trade." In M.M. Kostecki, ed., *State Trading in International Markets*. New York: St. Martin's Press.

Kostecki, M.M., ed. 1982. *State Trading in International Markets*. New York: St. Martin's Press.

Kraft, Daryl F., W. Hartley Furtan, and Edward W. Tyrchniewicz. 1996. *Performance Evaluation of the Canadian Wheat Board*. Report to the Canadian Wheat Board. Winnipeg: Canadian Wheat Board.

Marchildon, Greg P., and W. Hartley Furtan. n.d. "The 1993-94 Wheat War: Lessons for Canada-U.S. Relations?"

McCalla, A. F. 1996. "A Duopoly Model of World Wheat Pricing." *Journal of Farm Economics* 48: 711-27.

McCalla, A.F., and Andrew Schmitz. 1982. "State Trading in Grain." In M. M. Kostecki, ed., *State Trading in International Markets*. New York: St. Martin's Press.

Picketts, Valerie J., Andrew Schmitz, and Troy G. Schmitz. 1991. "The Potash Dispute." *American Journal of Agriculture Economics* 73: 255-65.

Schmitz, Andrew. 1996. *Economic Performance of the Canadian Wheat Board: Myth and Reality*. Report submitted to Brian H. Hay, Senior Counsel, Department of Justice, Government of Canada. Winnipeg.

Simonot, David Joseph. 1997. "An Examination of International State Trading in Wheat." Unpublished M.Sc. Thesis, University of Saskatchewan.

Tweeten, Luther. 1970. *Foundations of Farm Policy*. Lincoln: University of Nebraska Press.

United States General Accounting Office (GAO). 1997. *U.S. Agriculture Exports: Strong*

Growth Likely But U.S. Export Assistance Program's Contributions Uncertain. Report to the Chairman of the Committee on the Budget, House of Representatives. Washington: GAO.

_____. 1996. *Canada, Australia and New Zealand: Potential Ability of Agricultural State Trading Enterprises to Distort Trade.* Report to Congressional Requesters. Washington: GAO.

Western Grain Marketing Panel. 1996. *The Western Grain Marketing Panel Report.* Winnipeg.

Western Producer. 1997. (9 October).

Winnipeg Free Press. 1994. (25 January).

World Trade Organization (WTO) Secretariat. 1995. *Operations of State Trading Enterprises As They Relate to International Trade.* Background Paper by the Secretariat. WTO.

Countervailing and Antidumping Actions: An Evaluation of Canada's Experience with the United States

LARRY MARTIN, VINCENT AMANOR-BOADU, and
FIONA STIRLING

Introduction

As is well known, Canada and the U.S. are each other's principal trading partners. Between 1980 and 1988, the average annual total value of trade in all goods and services (imports plus exports) between Canada and the U.S. averaged $103 billion per year. As a result of the 1989 Canada-U.S. Trade Agreement (CUFTA), the total trade between the two countries had reached $290 billion by 1996. Canada's total trade with the rest of the world amounted to less than 29 percent of its total trade with the U.S. alone between 1989 and 1996. This indicates the importance of the smooth movement of goods and services between the two countries and, as well, Canada's particular dependence on this trading relationship. With reference to agrifood trade, the situation is not different from the trade in all goods and services. For example, U.S. total agrifood trade with Canada accounted for more than 17 percent of all its agrifood trade, while total Canadian agrifood trade with the U.S. averaged about 52 percent over the 1989 to 1996 period. Thus, this trade is of key importance for each country. Given this, any trade disruptions between Canada and the U.S. represent a significant cost to businesses in the two countries.

An overriding objective of international trade laws is to ensure that exporting nations do not obtain unfair advantage over domestic producers in importing countries. Therefore, most countries have developed their laws to ensure that the trade environment is fair and operates to enhance the value that consumers receive from traded goods and services. A review of the important components of U.S. and Canadian trade laws indicates some significant differences between the letter of the law in each country. It is important to note that the differences do not end with the letter but go also to the spirit and enforcement of the laws. These differences have subjected U.S.-Canada trade disputes to considerable academic analysis over the past two decades, as supported by the number and variety of papers and articles written on the subject (van Duren and Martin 1989; Martin 1991; Lermer and Klein 1990).

The two major types of trade dispute that have received the most attention and, certainly, have been used most by the U.S. against Canada are countervailing duties and antidumping actions. While significant work has been done on these, there is a need to revisit the issues within the framework of the emerging rules on dispute settlement mechanisms under multilateral trade agreements such as the North American Free Trade Agreement (NAFTA) and the World Trade Organization (WTO) (Meilke and van Duren 1990; Schmitz and Sigurdson 1990). This paper, therefore, proceeds with two objectives in mind: first, to evaluate Canada's experience with the U.S. with respect to countervail and antidumping cases over the years to determine their impact on trade relations between the two countries and, second, to assess the contribution of NAFTA and WTO to the improvement of trade dispute settlement between Canada and the U.S.

Two methods have been used here: a review of the trade literature, focusing on the economic synthesis of trade disputes, and an analysis of the agrifood-related trade disputes brought by the U.S. against Canada, focusing on countervail and antidumping cases. In addition, we present a brief explanation of the salient characteristics of countervail and antidumping under U.S. trade remedy laws and, in the section following that, we look at some examples of agrifood countervail and antidumping cases brought by the U.S. against Canada from the early 1980s and their resulting decisions. The paper concludes with a review of the changes introduced into international trade disputes by the GATT/WTO dispute settlement mechanisms and their implications on the certainty of trade and cost to business and industries.

Antidumping under U.S. Trade Remedy Laws

In a competitive market, international product prices are technically established by adding the cost of production of the product to the transportation cost involved in exporting the product, plus all additional charges such as duties and excise taxes. From that perspective, it is plausible to assume that the export price of a product cannot be lower than its domestic price. Dumping is said to have occurred when the price of a product in the importing country is less than in the exporting country. It is viewed as exporting products at a "loss" if the domestic market price is assumed to be "fair." U.S. trade remedy law presents three provisions for addressing different types of dumping. The Antidumping Act (1916) provides for criminal and civil penalties for the sale of imports at prices substantially lower than actual market value or wholesale price. The act has a criminal component because it addresses the intent of the pricing of the product: it is considered criminal if the intent of dumping is to destroy or injure a particular U.S. industry in its domestic market. Its successor, the Tariff Act (1930) provides for the assessment and collection of antidumping duties by the U.S. government when dumping is determined to have occurred. Section 731 of this act provides for the imposition and collection of antidumping duties, in addition to any other duties, if two conditions are met: First, the U.S. Department of Commerce (DOC) must determine that "a class or kind of foreign merchandise is being, or is likely to be, sold in the United States at less than its fair value." And, second, the U.S. International Trade Commission (USITC) must determine that an industry in the United States is "materially injured, or is threatened with material injury, or the establishment of an industry in the United States is materially retarded, by reason of imports of the merchandise." If these two conditions are established by the U.S. DOC and the USITC, then an antidumping order is issued against the exporter equal to the dumping margin—that is, the difference between foreign and the U.S. market value for the product.

The USITC determines the existence and extent of material injury prior to the imposition of antidumping duties. Section 77(17) of the Tariff Act (1930) defines material injury as "harm which is not inconsequential, immaterial or unimportant." The USITC uses a two-pronged approach to the establishment of material injury. First, it analyzes the effect of dumped product imports on U.S. prices of like products and, second, it analyzes effects of dumped imports on U.S. producers of like products, accounting for such factors as lost sales, market share, profits, productivity, return on investment, and production capacity utilization. It is also required to consider such factors as wages and employment, inventories, and development of the affected U.S. industry. A third provision falls under Section 1317 of the Omnibus Trade and Competitiveness Act (1988) which established procedures for the U.S. Trade Representative to request foreign governments to take action against third-country dumping that injures U.S. industry in that country. Thus, if the U.S. determines that dumping in another country injures a particular U.S. industry, it can request the importing country to impose an antidumping measure on the "offending" country. The U.S. allows itself other recourse if the import-ing country does not respond to its request.

Antidumping and Countervail under U.S. Trade Remedy Law

Under the Tariff Act, the importation of any products that have benefited from a subsidy may be subjected to the imposition of duties, referred to as countervailing duties. They are meant to offset any benefits accorded the imported product in the U.S. market due to the subsidy in the export market. Thus countervailing duties focus on subsidies that of-fer competitive advantage to imports.

How did the U.S. define "subsidies" under its trade remedy laws? Prior to the signing of the Uruguay Round of GATT and its successor agreement, WTO, countries were left to define subsidies to suit their situ-ation. As such, and in the case of Canada's experience with U.S. countervailing duty law, the definitions of subsidies used were those of the United States. According to Section 1312 of the Omnibus Trade and Competitiveness Act, subsidy includes, but is not limited to, the provi-sion of capital, loans, or loan guarantees on terms inconsistent with com-mercial considerations; the provision of goods or services at preferential rates; the grant of funds or debt forgiveness to cover operating losses sus-tained by a specific industry; or the assumption of any manufacture, pro-duction, or distribution costs or expenses (Library of Parliament 1989). Additionally, Section 613 of the Trade and Tariff Act (1984) also defines upstream subsidies. These are subsidies paid by a government with respect to an input used in the production of the subject product.

The amendments in the Tariff Act require that an injury test be conducted in the case of disputes with countries who signed the GATT Agreement Relating to Subsidies and Countervailing Measures (Subsi-dies Code) or countries with equivalent obligations, while those nonsignatory countries are not afforded the injury test. With the excep-tion of the injury test, the requirements of the countervailing duty law are the same for the two groups of countries.

From the above definitions of subsidies, it seems that U.S. countervailing duties could be applied only where subsidies are specific to an industry or geographic region, and not when they are "generally available" to all industries and all regions in the country. However, this is not what has prevailed in most countervail cases that the U.S. has brought against Canada. Also, U.S. law does not recognize the provision of the GATT Subsidies Code that injury to the domestic industry must be shown "to result from the effect of the subsidy." Figure 1 illustrates the process used in both countervailing duty and antidumping cases in the U.S.[1] The figure shows that termination of a case by USITC for having no legally sufficient basis for investigation does not prevent the U.S. DOC from continuing its investigation of either subsidies or less-than-fair value, as the case may be.

Figure 1: Schematic Outlay of Investigation and Decision Process for Countervailing Duties and Antidumping Cases in the U.S.

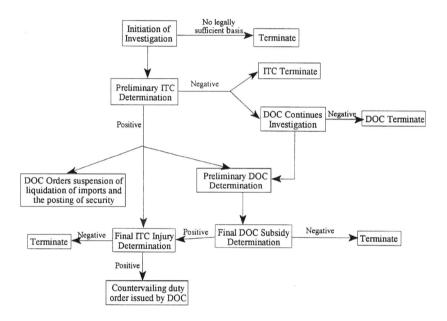

U.S. Agrifood Trade Actions against Canada

A selection of the cases that the U.S. brought against Canada under countervailing duty law and under antidumping law, seen in view of their internal consistency with U.S. trade remedy law, and their outcomes, illustrates the case.

Perhaps not surprisingly, the U.S. has used countervailing action more than any other nation, launching about 308 cases between 1980 and 1987 (DFAIT 1993). This represented more than 90 percent of all countervailing duty cases brought by all the GATT signatories together.

The U.S. brought a total of seventeen countervailing duty actions against Canada between 1980 and 1992. They covered government initiatives ranging from agricultural stabilization programs to government equity infusions. Their outcomes: 47 percent affirmative, 29 percent negative, and 24 percent terminated. Thus, in its countervail cases against Canada, the U.S. was successful less than half the time. Four of these seventeen cases were in agriculture and were brought between 1984 and 1989, the year CUFTA was implemented. Three of the cases were affirmative; the fourth was terminated. Table 1 shows the preliminary and final decisions associated with each of the four agriculture-related countervail cases against Canada.

Table 1: U.S. Agrifood Related Countervailing Cases against Canada

Year	Case	Preliminary Decision		Final Decision	
		ITC	ITA	ITC	ITA
1984	Live swine and pork	Affirmative (swine only)	Affirmative	Affirmative (swine only)	Affirmative
1985	Red Raspberries	Affirmative	Affirmative	Suspended	Terminated
1986	Cut Flowers	Affirmative	Affirmative	Affirmative	Affirmative
1989	Fresh, chilled, and frozen pork	Affirmative	Affirmative	Affirmative	Affirmative

Source: Chapman, Anthony. *Canada-U.S. Trade Disputes.* 1995.

Due to the notoriety of the hog and pork cases, as well as showing the various definitions of subsidies that the U.S. often applied to suit its cases, we here examine the live swine and pork case, as well as the fresh, chilled, and frozen pork case, more critically. These cases, technically speaking, were a single case that was divided when U.S. interests failed in their own courts to get an affirmative decision in the first place, but its details suggest a good deal about the U.S. approach to such matters. The value of live swine and pork imports from Canada to the U.S. in the early 1980s was estimated to be about $200 million per year. The Live Swine and Pork case was initiated by the International Trade Administration (ITA) in 1984. The International Trade Administration determined in 1985 that Canadian hog producers, but not pork processors, benefited from about twenty-two federal and provincial programs that qualified as subsidies. Subsequently, countervailing duties were levied on Canadian hog exports to the U.S. Investigations by USITC focused on Canada's federal

Agricultural Stabilization Act (ASA) payments, because they were targeted to specific industries, the specific rates varied from industry to industry, and there was government discretion in various stabilization schemes (DFAIT 1993). Additionally, the USITC observed that loan guarantees, interest payment assistance, and grants to defray transportation costs for hogs to processing facilities were all countervailable. Under the live swine and pork case, the U.S. held programs that covered more than one industry to be countervailable on condition that these programs differed in their treatment of the different industries they covered. This challenged its own "general availability" criterion for assessing subsidies, leading to the perception in Canada (and in other countries that suffered the U.S. changing definitions) that, as "prosecutor, judge, and jury," the U.S. was prepared to meet its trade protection objectives as legally as its laws permitted it to. At the same time, the ITC determined that the injury was caused only by imports of live hogs and not by imports of pork.

The decision was appealed in 1985 by the Alberta Pork Producers Marketing Board. The court supported the USITC determination that these imports "materially injure or threaten to injure" the U.S. industry. The U.S. Department of Commerce conducted final results of both the 1988-89 and 1989-90 administrative reviews of the Live Swine case after an appeal by the Canadian and provincial governments and Canadian producers in 1991. In both cases, the panel affirmed in part and remanded in part the agency determinations about which government programs were countervailable.

In 1988 the U.S. passed the Omnibus Trade and Competitiveness Act, which included a clause (written, we are told, by counsel for the U.S. pork interests) essentially directing the ITC to find injury from "upstream subsidies," such as those for Canadian hogs, for a downstream product, such as pork. The following year, U.S. interests brought the second case against imports of Canadian fresh, chilled, and frozen pork. Following the process ordained in the Omnibus Trade Act, USITC did not find that there was material injury from these imports, but did find that there was threat of material injury. This case was interesting because it was the first USITC determination to be appealed under the dispute settlement mechanism of the CUFTA by the Canadian federal and provincial governments in 1989. The CUFTA panel unanimously remanded the USITC determination. Following a second unanimous panel decision, the agency reversed its determination. The U.S. government, in turn, appealed the CUFTA panel decision through an Extraordinary Challenge Committee

(ECC) proceeding. The appeal was unanimously dismissed for failing to meet the extraordinary challenge criteria set out in the corresponding CUFTA Article and the ECC affirmed the panel decision and order.

Turning to antidumping trade actions, between 1980 and 1992 the U.S. initiated twenty-seven antidumping trade actions against Canada. Three of these were in agriculture. Thirteen of the twenty-seven cases were ruled affirmative, thirteen negative, and one was terminated. One agricultural case was determined affirmative, the other two negative. Table 2 shows the three agricultural antidumping cases and their outcomes.

Table 2: U.S. Antidumping Cases Brought against Canada

Year	Case	Preliminary Decision		Final Decision	
		ITC	ITA	ITC	ITA
1982	French Fries (potatoes)	Negative	—	—	—
1983	Potatoes	Affirmative	Affirmative	Affirmative	Negative
1985	Red Raspberries	Affirmative	Affirmative	Affirmative	Affirmative

Source: Chapman, Anthony. *Canada-U.S. Trade Disputes*. 1995.

Red raspberries accounted for annual trade of about $10 million in the early 1980s. The antidumping duty investigation of red raspberries was initiated by the ITA in 1984. The investigation covered fresh and frozen raspberries packed in bulk containers and suitable for further processing. In its final determination, in 1985, the ITA concluded that the merchandise was being sold in the U.S. for less than fair market value. In 1987, the ITA initiated a second review of the antidumping order and examined the imports of four processors/exporters. The result was an affirmation of the original ITA decision. The Red Raspberries case was appealed in 1989 by three Canadian exporters. It is interesting to note that the Red Raspberries case was the first to be referred to a binational panel for review under Article 1904 of the Canada-U.S. Trade Agreement. The result of the investigation was a unanimous panel decision to eliminate the antidumping duties of two exporters. On second remand, the agency eliminated duties for two other exporters. The panel decision was once again unanimous.

Trade-Distorting Outcomes of U.S. Trade Actions and Differing Dispute-Settlement Systems

U.S. trade remedy laws are structured in a way that can have significant trade-distorting outcomes once a case is brought against an industry or business. For example, the laws require that once the USITC makes a positive preliminary determination of injury in a countervailing duty case or less-than-fair value determination, an order to suspend the liquidation of the products in question may be made by the Department of Commerce subject to the determination from the publication date of preliminary determination. It is also required under the laws to make the exporters post security in the form of a bond, cash deposit, or some other appropriate security for each subsequent importation of the product in question. These securities are based on a preliminary estimate of what the Department of Commerce believes the extent of injury to be. There is nothing in the laws to prevent the U.S. from establishing penalty levels that fundamentally prevent imports and, hence, protect the domestic industry not from unfair competition, but from international competition, period. Reviews of the hog and pork case seem to lend credence to this.[2]

The fact that the Department of Commerce has the ability to impose penalties—that is, sentences—before the trial is over is another point of interest. To ensure that the preliminary duties achieve the objective of protecting the domestic industry, these preliminary duties have usually been established at higher than necessary levels. This assertion is supported by the reductions awarded Canada in the fresh, chilled, and frozen pork case, where a five-cent per kilogram refund was ordered in the final decision. In many Canadian industries, therefore, U.S. trade remedy laws were seen as harassment instruments used by the USITC and the Department of Commerce to provide relief, albeit temporary, to U.S. industries whenever Canadians responded to strong market conditions in the U.S. In addition to the hog case described above, there was the case of durum wheat in 1995, in which the U.S., after using the EEP to get most of its durum wheat into the international market and creating a shortage in the domestic market thereby, put pressure on Canada to limit its durum exports to the U.S. Fortunately, the changed trade environment has contributed to increased transparency and introduced some sensibilities in how trade disputes are settled, giving industry stakeholders more confidence in their dealings with the U.S.

The signing of the CUFTA did not change the process for settling trade disputes between Canada and the U.S.; trade dispute settlement rules were still under U.S. law if the U.S. brought the case and under Canadian law if it was initiated by Canada.[3] The major change was with the appeals process that determined whether decisions by USITC were consistent with U.S. law, or decisions by the Canadian International Trade Tribunal (CITT) were consistent with Canadian law. There are significant differences between the trade laws of the two countries, which may explain why the U.S. cannot complain of "trade harassment" by Canada. One example of the differences between the two systems is that it is much easier to instigate antidumping proceedings in the U.S. than it is in Canada. It is also easier to satisfy the requirements needed to support the complaint in the U.S. than in Canada, as Revenue Canada assesses each complaint on a three-fold basis: the allegations of dumping, the existence of alleged injury, and the causal connection between the dumping and the existence of injury. The Department of Commerce's assessment does not take into account injury or causality but depends on the USITC to do that. In Canada, a positive preliminary determination (for example, a finding of a margin of dumping or amount of subsidy) is an essential prerequisite for the continuation of investigative proceedings. The Department of Commerce, on the other hand, can continue investigations even if a negative preliminary determination has been made.[4]

The transparency of the investigation and injury assessment also differ significantly between the two countries. The CITT conducts a more transparent inquiry than does the USITC. Hearings in Canada can last up to three weeks, while USITC hearings are generally conducted in one day, with time limits for presentation and cross-examination. While both proceedings are adversarial, the CITT's process is more adjudicative, allowing for extensive cross-examination of domestic industry witnesses in Canada.

There are also differences in the scope of the investigation each country uses. In Canada, the scope is limited to the types of goods to which an injury can be demonstrated. The U.S., however, has broader product definitions, allowing their investigations, in turn, to be broader. Both countries rely on respondents to comply with questionnaires in order to gather industry data, but the U.S. Department of Commerce is more rigid in its approach towards data collection. This results in more instances of "best information available" being used by the DOC than by Revenue Canada, which can, in turn, result in more punitive duties. Differences in the final injury determination voting process also exist. The CITT, when hearing an antidumping or countervail case, generally sits in a panel of three. Decisions are made after the three members have deliberated on the evidence, and generally meet the objective of being unanimous. Since the Tribunal members sit in a panel of three, tie votes are not possible. In the U.S., decisions are rendered by six (or any even number of) commissioners. In the event of a tie vote, the domestic industry wins.

Costs for each of the administrating authorities and participants are higher under the U.S. system than they are in Canada. Both Revenue Canada and the Tribunal have fewer personnel dedicated to antidumping proceedings than do the Department of Commerce and the International Trade Commission. Also, the U.S. system requires participants to pay higher costs than those paid by participants in Canada; this is because the U.S. system has the USITC conduct a preliminary injury analysis, allowing counsel for the domestic industry to participate in the DOC's dumping investigation, and by requiring extensive written submissions, including experts' reports, during the final injury-determination stage. Another important difference between the two systems is enforcement. The U.S. system requires that bonds be posted during the provisional period and that deposits be made after an affirmative injury finding. The Department of Commerce decides, on a retrospective basis, after the finding, whether the amount of deposits is sufficient to cover any antidumping liability. Revenue Canada, on the other hand, permits the avoidance of payment of antidumping duties through the provision of prospective guidelines for pricing exports into Canada.

The Canadian system also provides for a sunset mechanism for reviewing findings which have been in place approximately five years, although findings can also be rescinded any time during the five-year period if the offending behavior is stopped in the exporting country. The U.S. has no such mechanism in place, although a sunset clause similar to Canada's has been adopted, effective 1 January 2000. In addition, as has been seen clearly in the pork case, reviews by the Department of Commerce of subsidy amounts take a very long time when the subsidy has been reduced, but occur quite quickly when the subsidy has been increased.

The above comparisons, summarized in Appendix A, reveal that many aspects of the U.S. system are more rigorous against both dumped and subsidized imports than Canada's. The Canadian system, however, has been more in line with prevailing GATT rules.

Trade Agreements and Changes in Trade Dispute Settlement Mechanisms

Both Canada and the U.S. have been signatories to international trade agreements that have contributed to the emerging dispute settlement processes. How are these trade agreements (CUFTA/NAFTA as well as the Uruguay Round and its successor WTO Agreement) contributing to the increasing confidence and transparency in international trade? The following sections address the dispute settlement mechanisms under the CUFTA/NAFTA and the GATT/WTO.

Both CUFTA and NAFTA use dispute settlement panels and these are assembled on a case-by-case basis, usually from a roster of people submitted by the disputing countries. Each party is entitled to select two panelists, and the fifth is named by agreement of the two parties. If no agreement is reached, the parties decide by lot which of them selects the fifth panelist. The panels are restricted to ruling on whether antidumping or countervailing duty determinations by the respective country's agencies are in accordance with domestic law and are directly applicable under Canadian and U.S. law. Thus, CUFTA and NAFTA did not depart from the application of domestic trade remedy laws, allowing for the inefficient U.S. system to be used even after CUFTA and NAFTA were signed.

In addition, both CUFTA and NAFTA provide for the establishment of an extraordinary challenge procedure, under which a party can, in limited cases, seek review of the binational review panel decision. The extraordinary challenge review is conducted by a three-member committee. Each of the parties chooses one member from a roster of sitting or formal judges, while the third member is chosen from the roster by the party designated by lot to choose the third committee member. The extraordinary challenge committee can review the proceedings of the binational panel to determine whether grounds exist to remand the panel, or whether the decision should be vacated and the case committed to a new panel. Grounds for reversal include:

- a member of the panel was guilty of gross misconduct, bias, a serious conflict of interest, or otherwise materially violated the established rules of conduct for panel proceedings;

- the panel seriously departed from a fundamental rule of procedure; and

- the panel exceeded its powers, authority, or jurisdiction.

Prior to the signing of the Uruguay Round of GATT, disputes settled by GATT were nonbinding on the disputants. This changed with the signing of the Uruguay Round and its successor agreement, WTO. There was, and still is, a strong encouragement of consultation to resolve disputes. Track II of the GATT Subsidies Code sets out an international dispute settlement process involving consultation, conciliation, and referral to a GATT panel of experts (Figure 2). If consultations fail and a

Figure 2: WTO Dispute Settlement Process

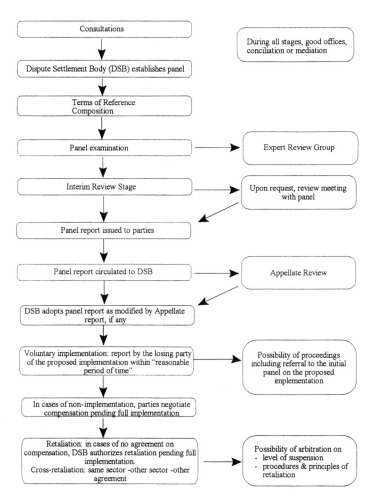

Source: WTO

mutually accepted solution is not reached in sixty days, a panel of informed people from countries not party to the dispute may be formed to investigate and make recommendations. The panel is comprised of three informed people, chosen from a roster of individuals with experience in the issues related to the agreement or who are experts in the field of trade or law. Panels are encouraged to report within six months, and recommendations are to be implemented within thirty days of receipt, unless one party gives notice of its intention to appeal or a consensus against the adoption of the report is reached.

In the event of an appeal, an Appellate Body consisting of individuals drawn from a roster will be formed. The Appellate Body has sixty days from the date when the party to the dispute gives formal notice of its intention to appeal. If the Appellate Body cannot provide its report within sixty days, it can inform the Dispute Settlement Body of the reasons for the delay. In no case can the appeal proceedings exceed ninety days. The appellate report is adopted by the Dispute Settlement Body and unconditionally accepted by the parties within twenty days of its issuance, unless the Dispute Settlement Body decides by consensus not to adopt the report.

If the recommendations are not implemented within six months from the date when the Dispute Settlement Board adopts either the panel report or the Appellate Body report, in the absence of agreement or compensation, the complaining party can suspend concessions with the approval of the Dispute Settlement Body. If it is determined that a subsidy or antidumping charge has caused injury, and the respective party has not taken appropriate steps to remove the adverse effects of the subsidy or withdraw the subsidy within the six-month period, the Dispute Settlement Body will grant authorization to the complaining party to take countermeasures, commensurate with the degree and nature of the adverse effects determined to exist. In the case of Canada and the U.S., any dispute that arises both under NAFTA and WTO can be settled in either forum at the discretion of the complaining party, although Mexico (the third party to NAFTA) must first be notified should the complaining party decide to have the dispute settled under WTO procedures. Should the two parties not agree under which forum settlement should take place, the dispute will normally be settled under NAFTA.

The WTO dispute settlement mechanism allows for an appeal by either party in a panel proceeding. The appeal, however, is limited to issues of law covered in the panel report, and the legal interpretation developed by the panel. Appeals are heard by a standing Appellate Body, which is established by the Dispute Settlement Body, and the Dispute Settlement Board adopts the report of the Appellate Body thirty days after it is issued. The Appellate Body report is unconditionally accepted by the parties to the dispute unless there is a consensus against adoption. Whether a case is appealed or not, the implementations of adopted recommendations or rulings are kept under surveillance by the Dispute Settlement Board until the issue is resolved.

Conclusion

Reviewing Canada's—and other countries'—experience with U.S. countervailing and antidumping cases in agriculture (and other sectors) shows why dispute settlement procedures have been one of the primary topics on Canada's agenda in bi-, tri-, and multilateral trade negotiations. The U.S. system of dispute settlement has been stacked somewhat in the interests of U.S. producers. At the same time, its rigor likely brought some discipline to the policies of exporting countries and the business practices of exporters. But the movement of responsibility for dispute settlement toward third parties with no vested interests in the outcome—such as binational panels and international quasi-courts, as is occurring under NAFTA and the WTO—likely brings even better discipline to export policies, exporters' behaviors, and to the dispute settlement process itself. One very positive implication of this transformation of the dispute settlement process is that, over time, there should evolve a consistent set of decisions and precedents that will allow better policy decisions, business behavior, and outcomes. The whole, as well, will be better defined. The former system, with each country having its own settlement process, could do nothing more than add confusion. As the world becomes smaller and trade becomes more important, there is a need to develop a single, global set of acceptable and unacceptable behavior by both governments and business. A centralized settlement process would facilitate this.

NOTES

1. In the case of countervail, the investigation at the U.S. Department of Commerce is on subsidies while it is on Less Than Fair Value (LTFV) in the case of antidumping.

2. See Meilke and van Duren (1990), van Duren and Martin (1989), and Schmitz and Sigurdson (1990).

3. The following is a summary taken from Remarks of the Hon. Donald S. Macdonald to the Special Joint Committees of Parliament Considering the Special Import Measures Act, 25 November 1996, Ottawa, by McCarthy-Tétrault.

4. See Figure 1 above.

REFERENCES

Chapman, Anthony. 1995. *Canada-U.S. Trade Disputes*. Ottawa: Research Branch, Library of Parliament.

Department of Foreign Affairs and International Trade. 1993. *U.S. Trade Remedy Law: A Ten-Year Experience*. Ottawa: Department of Foreign Affairs and International Trade.

Lermer, G., and K.K. Klein, eds. 1990. *Canadian Agricultural Trade: Disputes, Actions and Prospects*. Calgary: University of Calgary Press.

McCarthy-Tétrault. 1996. *Remarks of the Hon. Donald S. Macdonald to the Special Joint Committees of Parliament Considering the Special Import Measures Act*. Ottawa.

Meilke, K., and E. van Duren. 1990. "Economic Issues in the U.S. Countervail Case Against Canadian Hogs and Pork." In G. Lermer and K.K. Klein, eds., *Canadian Agricultural Trade: Disputes, Actions and Prospects*. Calgary: University of Calgary Press. 45-72.

Organization for Economic Cooperation and Development, Statistics Directories. 1995. *Foreign Trade by Commodities*. Paris: OECD.

Schmitz, A., and D. Sigurdson. 1990. "Stabilization Programs and Countervail Duties: Canadian Hog Exports to the United States." In G. Lermer and K.K. Klein, eds., *Canadian Agricultural Trade: Disputes, Actions and Prospects*. Calgary: University of Calgary Press. 73-92.

van Duren, E., and L. Martin. 1989. "Countervailing Disputes and Canadian Agriculture." *Canadian Public Policy* 2: 162-74.

World Trade Organization. "How the WTO Resolves Trade Disputes." http://www.wto.org/wto/dispute/webds.htm

APPENDIX: Summary of Differences between Canada and U.S. Trade Laws and Practice

	Current Canadian Law/Practice	Current U.S. Law/Practice
Transparency of the initiation process and the review of allegations contained in a complaint.	Revenue Canada generally performs a thorough analysis before initiating an investigation. The filing is not made public until satisfied that the complaint is properly documented (21 days) and that a *prima facie* case of dumping and injury, with a causal link between the two exists (additional 30-45 days).	Petitions are filed with both Commerce and Commission. The filing is a matter of public knowledge. Within 20 days of receipt of a petition (40 days if the industry is polled to assess support for the complaint) Commerce has to make a decision whether to initiate an investigation or not.
Investigative procedures used by Revenue Canada and Commerce.	Questionnaires are sent at the time of initiation of the investigation. Revenue Canada also conducts on-site verification and supplementary requests for information before the making of a Preliminary Decision.	Detailed and extensive questionnaires are sent out, with a call for a response within 30 days. The questionnaires require complete compliance. On-site verification, when undertaken, is based on rigid guidelines.
Involvement of Counsel.	Respondents are permitted to have the benefit of counsel during the investigative process. Counsel are made privy to as much information as a respondent authorizes.	Commerce, in addition to permitting counsel for the respondents access to their administrative record, also allows petitioner's counsel access provided they have been issued a protective order to maintain confidentiality.
Disclosure of methodology for dumping margin calculations used for Preliminary Determination purposes.	Respondents are provided with detailed disclosure of the results, including the methodology for the dumping calculations. Counsel is only able to determine the outcomes from publicly announced results and the statement of reasons accompanying the determination.	Disclosure of the results of the Preliminary Determination are made to the respondents and to all counsel subject to protective orders. *Continued on following page*

	Current Canadian Law/Practice	Current U.S. Law/Practice
Best information available.	If information provided was inadequate or did not meet verification requirements, a Ministerial Prescription specifying dumping margins based on best information available will be used.	Commerce will also use best information available determination if required.
Undertakings, termination, and suspension agreements.	Revenue Canada may accept undertakings which can result in a suspension of an investigation but only after a Preliminary Determination has been made. Undertakings can be terminated if Revenue Canada is so advised by any interested party within 30 days of acceptance of an undertaking. Violations of undertakings will result in their termination.	Commerce may suspend an investigation if the exporters who account for substantially all of the merchandise agree to (i) cease exports to the U.S. within 180 days, (ii) promptly revise their prices, and (iii) to eliminate the injurious effect of the imports in question. Investigation can also be terminated if the petitioner withdraws the petition, provided Commerce determines such withdrawal is in public interest.
The final injury determination— procedures.	The CITT's final assessment of injury is carried out in the context of an adversarial adjudicative-type oral hearing process, which can last from one to three weeks. The bulk of time is spent cross-examining witnesses on prior submitted written testimony.	Extensive oral hearings are not held by the Commission, although questioning of witnesses is permitted (but discouraged). Most hearings are completed in one day, with the Commission relying on staff investigations and the written representations made by interested parties. The investigative process continues after the hearing process, and decisions can be rendered based on information not available at the time of the hearing.

Continued on following page

	Current Canadian Law/Practice	Current U.S. Law/Practice
The final injury determination— the voting process.	Decisions are rendered by a panel (the Tribunal), generally made up of three individuals. Decisions are made after the three members have deliberated on the evidence, and are issued no later than 120 days after the Preliminary Determination. Written reasons are issued within 15 days of the decision.	Decisions are rendered by six (or any even number) individual Commissioners. In the case of a tie-vote, the domestic industry wins.
The injury finding—causal connection.	The causal connection requirement is taken very seriously. Each factor allegedly causing injury is weighed to determine the importance to be given to each. Dumping, regardless of other factors, is also analyzed. The degree of dumping, both in volume and margin, is also taken into account.	The existence of an industry's ill health and dumped imports are the only grounds necessary to making a decision. The determination process in finding dumping the cause of injury is not consistent among all Commissioners.
The injury finding— cumulation.	Cumulation permits the Tribunal to assess the impact of all dumped imports "en masse" in order to establish a causal connection between dumping and material injury. Cumulation is restricted to cumulating import volume and price data from two or more countries being simulta-neously investigated.	The Commission is required to cumulatively assess the volume and effect of imports (of subject merchandise) from all countries if such imports compete with each other and domestic like products in the U.S. market. Cumulations between investigations commenced separately at different time periods, and cross-cumulation between anti-dumping and countervail investigations is also permitted. *Continued on following page*

	Current Canadian Law/Practice	Current U.S. Law/Practice
Enforcement/ administrative reviews.	It is generally possible for importers to avoid paying provisional and final duties by increasing price levels equal to, or in excess of, prescribed "normal values." The normal values are provided by Revenue Canada.	The U.S. system is retrospective. Importers are required to post bonds during the provisional period for the estimated antidumping duties. Deposits are also required subsequent to the provisional period. Deposit rates may be changed in subsequent reviews. If collected deposit amounts are deemed insufficient, additional duties may be collected.
Sunset clause.	The Tribunal may review a material injury finding at any time, either on its own initiative or by request. As a result of the review, an order or finding can be made. The finding can be rescinded or continued with or without amendments. The Tribunal has to initiate a review by five years from the date of an order.	The U.S. has adopted a sunset clause similar to Canada's, to be effective as of 1 January 2000.

Integration and Interdependence in the U.S. and Canadian Live Cattle and Beef Sectors

LINDA M. YOUNG and JOHN M. MARSH

Introduction

The live cattle and beef markets of Canada and the United States are well integrated and highly interdependent, but this alignment occurs in an unequal fashion. Following this relation, the present paper assesses the role of trade agreements and domestic policies in increasing market integration and, also, analyzes the impact of remaining barriers to integration. This integration is necessarily accompanied by interdependence between the U.S. and Canadian livestock sectors and has associated costs and benefits. Discussing these issues, we use integration in the context of forming or blending markets into a whole—implying a certain degree of harmony. Criteria used to assess the degree of integration between the live cattle and beef markets include the following:

—prices in the two countries moving together (technically speaking, becoming cointegrated) so that a shock in one output market is transmitted to the other output market via supply and demand adjustments, and prices differ between points by transportation costs;

—trade occurring between the two countries; and

—similarities existing in important markets for inputs—in this case, feed.

For market integration to occur, the commodity in question must be relatively homogeneous, or without large differences in quality characteristics between the two countries. Integration of two countries' markets for a particular commodity—in this case, live cattle and beef—is prevented by the existence of trade barriers, including tariffs, quotas, and border regulations. Creation of an integrated market for live cattle and beef is also influenced by factors affecting supply and demand in each country. These factors include health and safety regulations, macroeconomic policies, and domestic agricultural and trade policies that affect commodity production and marketing and the cost of inputs such as feed grain. This paper begins with a discussion of trade agreements between the United States and Canada, the current level of integration of the U.S. and Canadian live cattle and beef markets, and resulting trade in live cattle and beef.[1] It then assesses remaining barriers to market integration.

Trade in Live Cattle and Beef Provisions of CUFTA

When the Canada–United States Free Trade Agreement (CUFTA) was implemented in 1989, tariffs on both live cattle and beef were reduced and, within a few years, many were eliminated altogether.[2] Since tariff

Figure 1: U.S. and Canadian Trade in Live Cattle

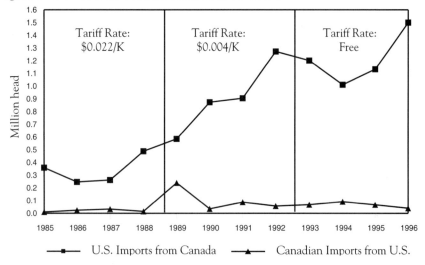

Figure 2: U.S. Production, Consumption, and Trade of Cattle, 1992-1996

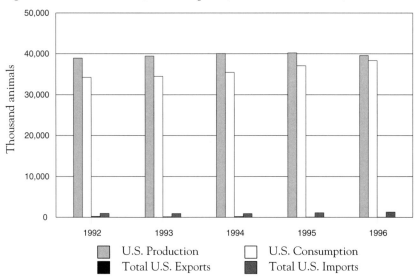

Figure 3: Canadian Production, Consumption, and Trade in Cattle, 1992-1996

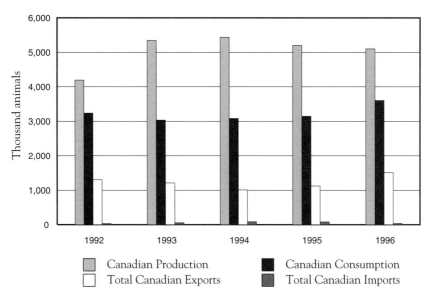

reductions were already in place, the implementation of the North American Free Trade Agreement (NAFTA) beginning in 1994 had little impact on trade between Canada and the United States, as the provisions from CUFTA were largely incorporated into NAFTA.

In 1996, the United States imported 1.5 million head of slaughter and feeder cattle from Canada, nearly a sixfold increase in the number of cattle imported prior to CUFTA, which numbered 262,091 in 1987 (see Figure 1). However, live cattle imports are still extremely small compared to the U.S. market, with imports of live cattle in 1996 (carcass weight equivalent) constituting around 4 percent of U.S. beef consumption. Figures 2 and 3 show production, consumption, and trade of live cattle for the United States and Canada. The United States exported 40,722 head of live cattle to Canada in 1996, which is less than 1 percent of 1997 Canadian consumption. Figure 1 illustrates trade in live cattle between the two countries and changes in tariff regimes. It is likely that changes in the tariffs were not extremely important in determining trade levels, as tariffs were already quite small at the beginning of the CUFTA. In 1988, the U.S. tariff on live cattle imports from Canada was 2.2 U.S. cents/ kilogram, just 1.4 percent on an *ad valorem* basis. The elimination of quotas may have been more important than reductions in tariffs in increasing

Figure 4: U.S. Boxed Beef Imports from and Exports to Canada, 1985-1996

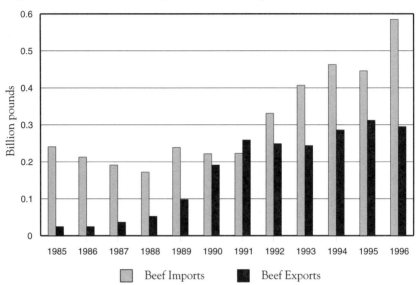

Beef Imports ▪ Beef Exports

trade between the United States and Canada. Before the CUFTA, each country restricted imports under their domestic meat import laws. With the CUFTA, these quotas were eliminated for trade between the United States and Canada.

U.S. and Canadian trade in beef is illustrated in Figure 4. U.S. imports of beef from Canada increased from 241 million pounds in 1985 to 586 million pounds in 1996. Even with this increase, imports of beef from Canada equaled just 2.3 percent of 1996 U.S. production. The United States is a much more important market for Canada than vice versa, with 60 percent of Canada's beef exports destined to the United States in 1996, but only 16 percent of U.S. beef exports destined to Canada. In 1996, 25 percent of Canada's beef production was exported, and imports equaled 23 percent of production. Figures 5 and 6 show production, consumption, and trade of beef for the United States and Canada. Measured in terms of beef production, the U.S. industry is ten times larger than Canada's and is less dependent on trade. In 1996, only 7 percent of U.S. production was exported, while beef imports represented 8 percent of U.S. production.

As impediments to trade between Canada and the United States were removed, north-south trade increased. Live cattle have been exported from the western provinces of Canada, particularly Alberta, to

Figure 5: U.S. Production, Consumption, and Trade of Beef, 1992-1996

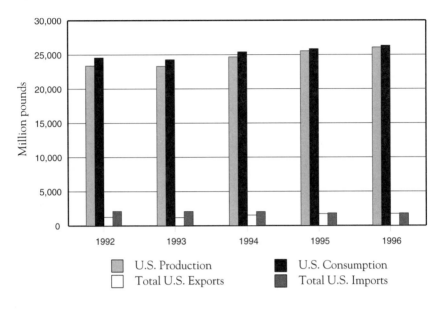

Figure 6: Canadian Production, Consumption, and Trade of Beef, 1992-1996

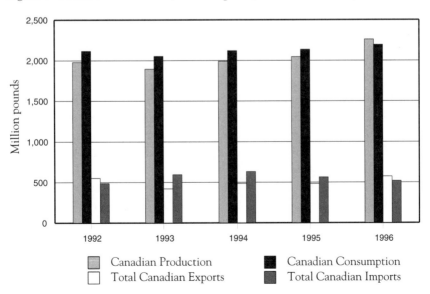

otherwise underutilized feedlots and packing plants in the western United States. Leading destinations include the states of Washington, Colorado, and Utah (U.S. International Trade Commission 1997). As the feedlot and packing industries in Alberta expand, it is anticipated that fewer Canadian slaughter cattle will be exported to the United States. In fact, U.S. feeder cattle are likely to be exported to Alberta. More Canadian beef is likely to be exported to the United States and to the Pacific Rim, also a major export market for the United States. Beef is exported from the midwestern United States into the eastern population centers in Canada. One reason for this long-established trade pattern is the long distance from Alberta to eastern Canada, between forty and fifty hours by road, whereas the midwestern United States is closer (Hayes, Hayenga, and Melton 1996).

Cattle and Beef Production in the United States and Canada

Cattle are raised throughout the United States; however, cattle operations are concentrated in the western rangelands, the corn belt, and the southeastern states where forage is abundant (U.S. International Trade Commission 1997). Between 1992 and 1996, the number of operators (defined as farms having one or more head) declined by 3 percent to 1.2 million. Many of these are family-owned and are part of diversified farming operations. The larger feedlots are concentrated on the west coast, in the southwest, and the southern plains and account for 83 percent of fed cattle marketings. The slaughter industry is the most highly concentrated, with 812 federally inspected plants in 1996. Four firms accounted for 81 percent of steer and heifer slaughter in 1994.

The western provinces of Alberta, Manitoba, Saskatchewan, and British Columbia accounted for two-thirds of the Canadian cattle inventory in 1997, with Alberta alone accounting for 38 percent. In 1996, of the 276,548 census farms in Canada, more than one-half raised cattle, producing cash receipts of $4.5 billion for cattle and calves (Ducksworth 1997). Expansion of two major cattle slaughtering facilities in Alberta (the Lakeside facility owned by Iowa Beef Processors and the High River facility owned by Cargill) will increase Alberta's slaughter capacity by one-third. Concentration of the slaughter industry in Canada is similar to that found in the U.S. industry. In 1996, four packing plants (three located in Alberta) accounted for 80 percent of Canadian cattle slaughter (Jewison 1997).

Agricultural Policies Affecting Cattle and Beef Production

This section describes the agricultural policies that have affected beef and veal production in the two countries and discusses trends in government subsidization of the industry. Figure 7 shows producer subsidy equivalents for Canada and the United States for beef and veal for the years 1984 to 1992 (Economic Research Service 1994). Producer subsidy equivalents are the sum of specified government subsidies to the sector as a percentage of commodity receipts. Producer subsidy equivalents for Canada are significantly higher than for the United States, at times twice as high, although the level of support for beef and veal is lower than that for other commodities. Although producer subsidy equivalents are a useful summary measure for comparing the degree of intervention over time, they are acknowledged to be an imperfect measure of subsidization. It is useful to keep in mind that the degree of government intervention, as measured by producer subsidy equivalents, does not address the degree of distortion that these policies cause in production and consumption decisions.

Many U.S. and Canadian policies affecting beef and veal production are similar, and subsidies measured in the producer subsidy equivalents are shown in Figure 8. Both the United States and Canada protect their domestic industries through tariffs, although this protection will decline moderately with the implementation of the 1994 Uruguay Round

Figure 7:   U.S. and Canadian Producer Subsidy Equivalents for Beef and Veal, 1984-1992

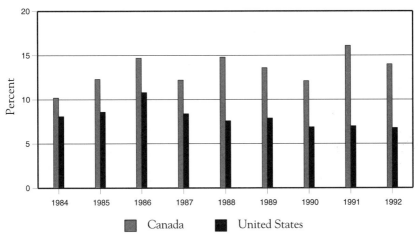

Agreement (WTO 1995).[3] Both countries subsidize their industries through provision of inspection services, research and advisory programs, and marketing and promotion programs, although the importance of these government policies varies between countries. In Canada, meat grading was privatized in 1996. The Canada Beef Grading Agency performs this function and is a nonprofit corporation that operates on a cost-recovery basis. In addition, both countries have allowed their cattle industries to use federal lands for grazing at prices that are less than market value.

Canada has eliminated a number of programs previously used to assist the beef industry. The National Tripartite Stabilization Program, an insurance program funded by the Canadian federal and provincial governments and producers, was eliminated in 1995 (Huff 1997). This program included two agreements for cattle: the cow-calf agreement and the slaughter cattle agreement. The major objective was to stabilize the receipts of participating beef producers by providing payments when the national average market price for beef fell below a calculated support price (U.S. International Trade Commission 1993).

In August 1995, the Canadian federal government eliminated transportation subsidies for Canadian grain bound for export. This grain freight subsidy is not included in Figure 8, which details subsidies for cattle and beef. However, programs used to offset distortions caused by grain transportation subsidies, including the Western Grain Transportation Authority Offset Program, the Feed Freight Assistance Program, and the Alberta Crow Benefit Offset Program were eliminated either prior to or concurrent with the grain transportation subsidies. Currently, the Net Income Stabilization Account is the only program providing whole farm net income stabilization, which affects both grain and cattle producers. However, the province of Alberta, which accounts for 60 percent of beef cattle production, has opted out of this program. It uses a separate program to stabilize farm incomes, the Farm Income Disaster Program (Govindasamy 1997).

The United States does not have a regular program of income support for stockgrowers. The United States does have several programs that promote beef exports. The U.S. Meat Export Federation is funded by industry and federal funds and promotes all U.S. meat exports. U.S. federal programs guarantee credit to importers, and market development programs provide a small level of assistance to U.S. meat exports (Ackerman, Smith, and Suarez 1995). To the extent that export promotion programs result in higher U.S. market prices, they may also increase U.S. imports of live cattle and beef from Canada. Overall, government intervention in the beef sector has been reduced over

Figure 8: Composition of U.S. and Canadian Producer Subsidies, 1984-92 (Average Percentage Shares*)

Canada		United States	
Property	%	Property	%
Feed Freight Asst. Program	1	Advisory	3
Marketing and Promotion	6	Pest and Disease Control	3
Development	9	Grazing Feed	3
ASA/Tripartite Payments	9	Beef Purchases	3
WGTA Offset Programs	10	Taxation	7
Tariffs	10	Research	8
Research, Advisory	12	Inspection	10
Inspection Services	17	Farm Credit	18
Provincial Programs	28	State Programs	19
		Tariffs	23

* Totals may not add up to 100% due to rounding

Source: Economic Research Service. *Estimates of Producer and Consumer Subsidy Equivalents: Government Intervention in Agriculture, 1982-1992.* U.S. Department of Agriculture, Statistical Bulletin No. 913 (Washington: USDA, 1994).

the last ten years, particularly in Canada which had much larger support programs. The programs remaining in Canada and in the United States have many similarities and are not likely to distort markets to a significant degree.

The United States and Canada have each had numerous and quite different policies affecting the production of feed grains. In the U.S., implementation of the 1996 Federal Agricultural Improvement Act (FAIR ACT) largely eliminates the linkage between planting decisions for grains and government payments to producers. This should increase the responsiveness of U.S. feed grain supply to price signals (Smith and Glauber 1997). The United States has not used export subsidies for grains since July 1995. Although export subsidies for wheat were more prevalent than those for barley, both resulted in an increase in the U.S. price of feed grains (Gray, Becker, and Schmitz 1995).

For its part, the Canadian government has delivered farm income support for grain producers through several programs and has made three *ad hoc* payments to grain producers. Currently, the only direct income support program is the Net Income Stabilization Account (NISA). Due both to the nature of NISA and its small size, it probably has a very small impact on grain production (Gray and Smith 1997). More pertinent for the livestock industry is the removal of transportation subsidies for grains, which is expected to decrease the price of feed grains in the prairie provinces and has been one factor behind the recent expansion in the feedlot and packing industries in Alberta. In a broad assessment of policies affecting grains, including income support, price policies, land retirement, and crop insurance, Gray and Smith note that the "pattern of reduced intervention in both countries has led to considerable economic convergence in grains and oilseeds programs implemented in the two countries" (Gray and Smith 1997, 16).

However, an important and contentious difference continues to exist in grain marketing. In Canada, the Canadian Wheat Board (CWB) has the sole authority to export wheat and barley. Thus, wheat and barley sales to the United States are determined by the CWB. The CWB also controls the sale of wheat and barley for human consumption in the Canadian domestic market. The single-desk seller status of the CWB is a controversial issue within Canada and has been the subject of a producer referendum, a recent court case, and an investigation by a federally appointed commission. Removal of the single-desk seller status of the CWB could influence feed grain prices both in Canada and in the United States and the quantity of feed grains exported from Canada to the United States. Empirical economic analyses of this question have reached different conclusions.

The question addressed by the following studies concerns the impact of the removal of the single-desk seller status of the CWB. Although consequences are much broader, only the price impacts on feed grains and Canadian export volumes to the United States are considered here. Schmitz et al. (1997) find that the price of feed barley would decline in the prairie provinces on average by Can$3.52/metric tonne (mt), a decline of about 2 percent (based on the Winnipeg 1995-96 average price for western feed barley of Can$168). They also estimate that export sales of feed barley by Canada would decrease by an average of 500,000 tons and that Canadian feed barley consumption would, on average, slightly increase. Both Carter (1993) and Johnson and Wilson (1995) conclude that exports of feed barley from Canada to the United States would increase if the authority of the CWB to control exports were removed. This would decrease U.S. feed prices, but the decrease would be extremely small. Carter finds that the price of feed barley would decrease in Canada as well, with the likely implication that more would be consumed by the Canadian livestock industry.

The U.S. livestock industry has expressed concern over the single-desk seller status of the Canadian Wheat Board (National Cattlemen and

Beef Association 1997). The U.S. National Cattlemen and Beef Association asked the Canadian Cattlemen's Association to help alleviate barriers prohibiting U.S. producers from directly purchasing barley from Canadian barley growers. They believe that Canadian barley is cheaper because of the single-desk seller status of the CWB; it provides Canadian cattle feeders with a $60 per head advantage on finishing costs. If this estimate is accurate, it would translate into a production cost advantage of $5.00 per hundredweight for a 1,200 pound slaughter steer.

Although empirical findings are dissimilar, the impact of a change in the level of imports of feed wheat and barley would be extremely small, due to the size of the feed grain market in the United States. For Canada, if feed barley prices declined as estimated in Schmitz et al., Canadian livestock production is estimated to increase by 2.4–4 percent if offsetting factors do not occur.

Degree of Market Integration

Prices for live cattle in the United States and Canada are illustrated in Figure 9. The data show that they move together and have the same turning points. Due to the large size of the United States market relative

Figure 9: U.S. and Canadian Slaughter Prices

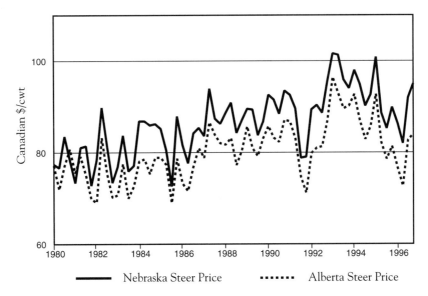

to Canada, it is commonly argued that cattle and beef prices are determined in the U.S. market, with Canadian prices reflecting differences in exchange rates and transportation costs. A statistical analysis of U.S. and Canadian slaughter prices was performed to further investigate this price relationship. Canadian slaughter prices were regressed on U.S. slaughter prices (converted into Canadian dollars, all nominal prices), over the period 1989-1996, using quarterly data. The results were:

(1) PcattleCanada = -4.55 + 0.97 PcattleUS R^2 = .89
    standard error   (5.63) (0.06)

An Augmented Dicky-Fuller Unit Root Test was performed on the residuals of Equation 1, and results indicated rejection of a unit root, with the conclusion that U.S. and Canadian slaughter prices are cointegrated. The coefficient of 0.97 on the U.S. cattle price indicates that the U.S. and Canadian cattle prices are highly correlated. This analysis could not be performed on beef prices due to lack of Canadian data (Dunford 1997).

The previous discussion of feed grain policies in the United States and Canada indicates that institutional barriers exist between these markets. The same empirical analysis was performed on Canadian feed barley prices and U.S. feed barley prices (converted into Canadian dollars). Again, quarterly data from 1989 to 1996 was used. Results are:

(2) PbarleyCanada = 1.03 + 0.70 PbarleyUS R^2 = .75
    standard error (0.18) (0.07)

An Augmented Dicky-Fuller Unit Root Test was performed on the residuals of Equation 2, and results indicated rejection of a unit root, with the conclusion that U.S. and Canadian barley prices are cointegrated. The correlation between U.S. and Canadian barley prices is lower than for live cattle and the R^2 barley is lower than for the equation for live cattle, indicating that other variables are needed to explain the price of barley in Canada.

As Gardner (1997) points out, if the cointegrating relationship were perfect, the coefficient on the U.S. price would not be statistically different than one, and the intercept would exactly measure the spread between the two prices. Gardner notes that it is difficult to evaluate what causes departures from market integration, or if we should be impressed or unimpressed with the level of market integration. These caveats noted, these two equations do offer econometric evidence that U.S. and Canadian livestock and barley prices move together, and this is not simply due to the prices sharing a common trend.

Regulatory Policies Affecting Market Integration

Integration of the U.S. and Canadian live cattle markets was facilitated by a pilot project started in October 1997 to reduce sanitary regulations at the border. Sanitary requirements are of greater relative importance since the decline of other barriers to trade. Industry leaders from the province of Alberta and the state of Montana have promoted this change to make it less costly to move cattle across the border in either direction. Due to the expansion in the feedlot and packing industry in Alberta, Alberta is expected to import feeder cattle from U.S. northern-tier states.

The pilot project eliminates testing for anaplasmosis, brucellosis, and tuberculosis for U.S. feeder cattle imported into Canada for the period 1 October through 31 March (Young and Marsh 1997). There are strict identification requirements for feeder cattle imported under the pilot program, and these cattle cannot commingle with the Canadian herd. In turn, the United States eliminated federal test requirements for brucellosis and tuberculosis for Canadian cattle, and the state of Montana eliminated its vaccination requirement for brucellosis. This reduction applies only to Canadian cattle imported into the states of Montana and Washington; Canadian cattle moving to other states are subject to the full range of requirements.

Although the project will reduce the cost of moving Canadian cattle into Montana, it is not expected that many Canadian cattle will be exported to Montana as a final destination. Canada's insistence on a reciprocal decrease in border regulations is an attempt to be designated as brucellosis-free by the United States, a first step to the elimination of the brucellosis test on all Canadian cattle exported to the United States.

This pilot project is indicative of the kinds of changes that are likely to occur due to the Sanitary and Phytosanitary Agreements of both the Uruguay Round Agreement (URA) and NAFTA. These agreements are roughly similar. One new concept is that sanitary restrictions should be based on regions, not countries, when a disease is limited to, and can be confined within, a region. This regionalization concept, which is being advanced by the Animal Health and Plant Inspection Service of the United States (APHIS), applies to brucellosis, the incidence of which differs by state in the United States. For example, Montana has a very low incidence of brucellosis, and its proximity to Canada made it appropriate for implementation of the pilot project. The implementation of the pilot project will have a small but positive impact on the beef industry. By significantly reducing the costs of sending animals across the border, it will facilitate packer procurement of animals within a least-cost distance of their plants without reference to national borders. A reduction in net U.S. imports of live cattle from Canada due to Canadian feedlot and packing expansion should also mitigate the demands for protection in the United States.

The Sanitary and Phytosanitary Agreements of NAFTA and the URA also mandate that a country's regulations must be based on science and can be challenged if the regulations do not meet international standards. The implementation of these rules will have both costs and benefits for the industry. However, both Canada and the United States increasingly depend on export markets. A recovery in consumer confidence in livestock products may be facilitated by stricter implementation of sanitary rules based on scientific criteria rather than politics. Increased demand for livestock products in countries such as Japan and Korea would have a positive impact on prices in Canada and the United States.

Mutual recognition of the equivalency of U.S. and Canadian meat grading systems has not occurred. Although the systems are similar, some differences do exist. For example, the marbling standards for USDA Choice and Select are identical to those used in the Canadian AAA and AA grades respectively. However, differences exist between U.S. and Canadian grade standards in terms of maturity, meat color, muscling, and fat (Canadian Beef Grading Agency 1997). Lack of grading system equivalency has ramifications for U.S.-Canadian trade in beef, and the impacts were described and estimated by Hayes et al. in their 1996 study. Canadian packers are forced to sell boxed beef at greatly reduced prices in the United States, commonly called "no-roll prices," due to the lack of a USDA stamp. However, Canadian carcasses can be imported into the United States, fabricated, and receive USDA grades. This has resulted in lower boxed-beef exports to the United States and higher exports of carcasses than would occur with grade equivalency.

If grading barriers were removed, western Canada would export approximately 27,000 additional tons of beef to the United States, primarily boxed middle cuts of select and choice beef. Canadian packers sell more beef than they would otherwise to eastern Canada because of the large discount on sales to the United States. The same is true for U.S. packers. Because U.S. beef cannot be sold into the eastern Canadian market without a large reduction in price, the U.S. beef industry is deprived of a lucrative outlet for the lean beef that is preferred in eastern Canada. Hayes et al. estimate this cost to be equivalent to a 5 percent tax on U.S. beef that is exported to Canada.

The U.S. Department of Agriculture recently implemented new regulations, the Hazard Analysis Critical Control Points (HACCP), for meat and poultry processing and slaughter plants. HACCP is a system that identifies specific hazards that adversely affect the safety of food and identifies preventative measures for hazard control. All state and federally inspected meat and poultry slaughter and processing plants must have such a plan. Testing for salmonella on raw meat and poultry products and for generic *E. coli* on carcasses will be used to monitor effectiveness of the HACCP plan (Antle 1995; Crutchfield et al. 1997). Implementation dates for HACCP are based on plant size. Large plants, defined as those with 500 or more employees, are now required to test for *E. coli*. Other aspects of HACCP will be phased in; plants with 11–499 employees will be required to begin in January 1999, and plants with fewer employees will begin in the year 2000.

Research is currently being conducted on the impact of these food safety regulations on the cost structure of the U.S. industry (Antle 1997). Imposition of HACCP regulations is likely to increase the costs of the U.S. industry. If an equivalent set of regulations is not imposed on the Canadian industry, the U.S. industry may suffer a competitive cost disadvantage, with a resulting change in trade patterns. However, if U.S. meat ends up being safer, the United States could gain an advantage.

Industry Marketing Initiatives

The Canadian Cattlemen's Association is developing a national cattle identification system (Grogan 1997). The purpose of the system is to track the original source of an animal over its lifetime. Although the technology is still being developed, it may take the form of a small computer chip placed in the animal. Concerns over food safety, particularly those expressed by customers in Asian markets, have prompted this initiative to identify and correct the sources of disease.

The Canadian industry has also implemented a system to increase the accuracy of payments for quality characteristics of beef, a system called value-based marketing. For example, Western Feedlot in High River, Alberta, has a program with Cargill in which producers receive an initial payment based on 95 percent of the current calf market. After slaughter and grading, producers are paid premiums based on carcass quality. This system is new, and variations are being tried throughout Canada and the United States. Actions by the industry are indicative of the high degree of integration that exists in the live cattle market. Efforts have been made to launch a producer-owned beef processing and marketing cooperative named Northern Plains Premium Beef (Tjaden 1997). Although this cooperative is based in North Dakota, it has members from Canadian provinces.

Conclusions: Interdependence and Integration

Evidence indicates that the live cattle and beef industries of the United States and Canada are well integrated. Quotas and tariffs no longer restrict trade, and border sanitary restrictions are being reduced. Trade in both directions has increased since the implementation of the Canada-U.S. Free Trade Agreement. U.S. and Canadian slaughter cattle prices are closely related. Distortions caused by domestic policies affecting the beef sector still exist but have been significantly reduced over the past ten years, particularly in Canada. The grain marketing system in Canada prevents free movement of feed wheat and barley across the border. However, the impact of this institutional barrier on the livestock industry is likely to be small.

Although trade barriers have decreased in importance, differences in domestic regulations exist. Lack of equivalency in meat grading between the United States and Canada distorts trade flows between these countries and increases the quantity of Canadian exports of carcasses relative to beef. The implementation of new safety regulations in the United States, namely HACCP, may also affect trade by increasing costs in the U.S. industry.

The increasing level of integration in U.S. and Canadian cattle and beef markets has been accompanied by a corresponding increase in their interdependence. This interdependence has a number of ramifications. Policymakers in both countries must recognize that domestic and export policies need to account for open borders between the two countries. This severely limits the choice of policies available to achieve a particular policy goal. In addition, the government must continually defend the integrity of free trade agreements from domestic interests who argue for protection.

In the United States, there have been two recent investigations by the U.S. International Trade Commission on the impact of trade agreements on the level of imports, and thus on domestic prices.

There are positive aspects to interdependence as well. With open borders, industries on each side must be aware of innovations in marketing, including value-based marketing, identity preservation, and methods to add value to products. Transportation costs will always limit the choice of packers that producers can sell to. However, within these bounds, a single market means that there are more choices for producers. The beef industries in both the United States and Canada are increasingly dependent on export markets, particularly the Pacific Rim. Income growth and dietary changes toward more animal-source proteins will increase this dependence. Since the late 1980s, the United States has exported increasing amounts of choice and prime grade beef, particularly to Japan. However, Canada desires to seize opportunities here, perhaps more in terms of lean beef, as Asian consumers have increased their demand for lean beef. Thus, both countries have a mutual interest in increasing access to third-country markets. This is partially motivated by declining per capita consumption of beef in U.S. and Canadian domestic markets. Due to the relative size of the U.S. and Canadian markets, the interdependence between them is not equal. The Canadian industry has a higher degree of dependence on the U.S. market for its exports than vice versa and is vulnerable because the U.S. market is the major force in price determination.

Integration of U.S. and Canadian live cattle and beef markets is well advanced, and it is perhaps the most integrated market of the major agricultural commodities. Supply management of the Canadian dairy, egg, and poultry industries and the implementation of high tariffs after the removal of quotas have prevented integration in those markets. For grains, marketing institutions and systems in Canada prevent complete market integration. For cattle and beef, the lack of trade barriers and relative unimportance of government intervention in the sector have facilitated movement toward a single market.

NOTES

1. Beef in this context refers to both carcasses and table cuts.

2. Presidential Proclamation #6343, on 2 October 1991, implemented an accelerated schedule of duty eliminations under the Canada–United States Free Trade Agreement and made these changes retroactive to 1 July 1991 (USITC 1995). Tariffs

on live cattle were reduced from 2.2 cents/kilogram to 0.4 cents/kilogram in 1989, and tariffs were eliminated completely in 1993. Tariffs on most categories of fresh or chilled beef were reduced from 3.9 cents/kilogram in 1989 to 2.6 cents/kilogram in 1992 and were eliminated in 1993. The tariff on frozen boneless beef was 1.7 cents/kilogram in 1989 and was eliminated in 1993.

3. Under the Uruguay Round Agreement, Canada has a duty-free quota for imports of beef (fresh, chilled, and frozen) of 76,409 metric tons, product weight (World Trade Organization 1995). For amounts over the duty-free quota, an *ad valorem* tariff will decrease from 37.9 percent to 26.5 percent by the year 2000. The United States is committed to a low-duty quota for beef of 656,621 metric tons, with a possible increase of 40 metric tons for Argentina and Uruguay with satisfaction of U.S. sanitary requirements for uncooked beef. In-quota tariffs are $44 per ton for carcasses and half-carcasses, 4 percent for high-quality beef, and 10 percent for other processed beef. Over-quota tariffs will decline by 15 percent, from 31.1 percent to 26.4 percent, by the year 2000. Market access was increased for the United States under the URA, as in 1994 the trigger level of imports under the Meat Import Law was 552,900 metric tons.

REFERENCES

Ackerman, K., M. Smith, and N. Suarez. 1995. "Agricultural Export Program: Background for 1995 Farm Legislation." USDA Agricultural Economic Report No. 716, Washington.

Antle, J.M. 1995. *Choice and Efficiency in Food Safety Policy.* Washington: American Enterprise Institute.

_____. 1997. "Impacts of Food Safety Regulation on Structure and Competitiveness of the Meat and Poultry Slaughter Industry." Homepage, http//www.trc.montana.edu (10 October). Trade Research Center, Montana State University–Bozeman.

Canadian Beef Grading Agency. 1997. "Canadian Beef Carcass Grading Regulations." (12 February) Calgary.

Carter, C.A. 1993. "An Economic Analysis of a Single North American Barley Market." Report prepared for the Deputy Minister, Grains and Oilseeds Branch, Agriculture Canada, Ottawa (March).

Crutchfield, S., J. C. Buzby, T. Roberts, M. Ollinger, and C.T.J. Lin. 1997. "An Economic Assessment of Food Safety Regulations: The New Approach to Meat and Poultry Inspection." (July) Washington: Economic Research Service, U.S. Department of Agriculture, AER No. 755.

Ducksworth, B. 1997. "Producers Will Decide If They Want a Beef Levy." *Western Producer* 74 (3 July): 4.

Dunford, A. 1997. CANFAX, personal communication (9 September).

Economic Research Service. 1994. "Estimates of Producer and Consumer Subsidy Equivalents: Government Intervention in Agriculture, 1982–92." USDA Statistical Bulletin No. 913, Washington (December).

Gardner, B. 1997. "Canada/U.S. Farm Policies and the Creation of a Single North American Market." Paper presented at the conference *The Economics of World Wheat Markets: Implications for North America* (May). Trade Research Center, Montana State University-Bozeman.

Govindasamy, N. 1997. Alberta Agriculture, Food and Rural Development, personal communication (30 October).

Gray, R., T. Becker, and A. Schmitz, eds. 1995. *World Agriculture in a Post-GATT Environment.* Saskatoon: University of Saskatchewan Extension Press.

Gray, R., and V.H. Smith. 1997. "Harmonization and Convergence of Canadian and U.S. Grains and Oil Seeds Policies: 1985–1996." Policy Issues Paper No. 4, Trade Research Center, Montana State University-Bozeman (December).

Grogan, H. 1997. Canadian Cattlemen's Association, personal communication (29 October).

Hayes, D., M. L. Hayenga, and B. E. Melton. 1996. "The Impact of Grade Equivalency on Beef and Cattle Trade Between the U.S. and Canada." *U.S. Meat Export Analysis and Trade News* (February).

Huff, B. 1997. "Changing Role of Public Policy in Canadian Agriculture." Paper presented at the annual meetings of the American Agricultural Economics Association, Toronto (27-30 July).

Jewison, G. 1997. CANFAX, personal communication (November).

Johnson, D.D., and W.W. Wilson. 1995. "Border Dispute in the Barley Trade." In R. Gray, T. Becker, and A. Schmitz, eds., *World Agriculture in a Post-GATT Environment.* Saskatoon: University of Saskatchewan Extension Press.

National Cattlemen's Beef Association. 1997. "NBA Moves to Eliminate Canadian Barley Import Barriers." ogr/press_releases_hr_barl_ncba.html (14 October).

Schmitz, A., R. Gray, T. Schmitz, and G. Storey. 1997. "The CWB and Barley Marketing: Price Pooling and Single-Desk Selling."

Smith, V.H., and J. Glauber. 1997. "The Effects of the 1996 Farm Bill on Feed and Food Grains." Policy Issues Paper No. 3 (September). Trade Research Center, Montana State University-Bozeman.

Tjaden, T. 1997. "Beef Coop to Press Forward." *Western Producer* 3 (20 March).

U.S. International Trade Commission. 1993. " Live Cattle and Beef: U.S. and Canadian Industry Profiles: Trade and Factors of Competition." Publication No. 2591 (January). Washington.

U.S. International Trade Commission. 1997. "Cattle and Beef: Impact of the NAFTA and Uruguay Round Agreements on U.S. Trade." Publication No. 3048 (July). Washington.

Young, L.M., and John M. Marsh. 1997. "Live Cattle Trade Between the United States and Canada: Effects of Canadian Slaughter Capacity and Health Regulations." Research Discussion Paper No.7, Trade Research Center, Montana State University-Bozeman (December).

World Trade Organization. 1995. *International Bovine Meat Agreement Annual Report: Summary of the Results of the Uruguay Round in the Meat Sector* (February). Geneva.

Pressures and Challenges in Integrating the U.S.-Canada Grains Sector

WILLIAM W. WILSON and BRUCE DAHL

Introduction and Scope

For at least a decade, there have been pressures to evolve toward a more integrated grain-marketing system in North America.[1] This process has been fraught, however, with difficulties apparently related to incompatible institutional and policy regimes possessed by the two countries. Such differences have resulted in very difficult political situations, and these difficulties have evolved through commercially led pressures to harmonize the two countries' systems. But, due to the drastically different grain-marketing systems, commercial harmonization has been difficult as well—policy harmonization is also needed. Given these frictions, the purpose of this paper is to detail some of the pressures and to treat their likely evolution.

Reciprocal trade issues between the United States and Canada have been the topic of numerous previous inquiries and studies.[2] Of particular importance have been the U.S.-Canada Joint Commission on Grains, which had contributing papers by Gray and Gardner; Furtan and Abel; Wilson, Johnson, and Dahl; and Loyns and Kraut. Subsequently, and in response, Canada initiated its own internal inquiry to identify important changes for the future, particularly given changes within the North American marketing system. The Western Grains Marketing Panel's (WGMP) report examined all aspects of the marketing of western Canadian grains, oilseeds, and specialty crops. Other studies include those by Young, Kraft, et al. and The Exchange Group. Johnson and Wilson and Young addressed some of these issues, but in a broader context of policy differences, and Alston, Gray, and Sumner and Marsh and Johnson have analyzed price impacts of imports.

Grain Flows

Trade in wheat, barley, and oats between the United States and Canada largely flowed from Canada to the United States from 1990 to 1996 (Canada Grains Council 1996). These data are summarized in Figures 1-5. Canadian exports of wheat to the United States

Figure 1: Canadian Exports to the United States, 1990-96

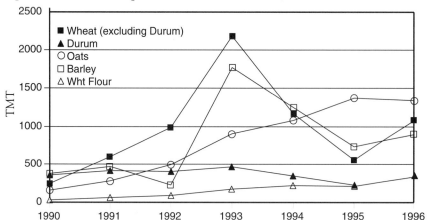

increased from 290 thousand metric tonnes (*tmt*) in 1990 to 2,172 *tmt* in 1993. Since 1993, wheat exports declined to near 564 *tmt* in 1995 and were up to 955 *tmt* in the first ten months of 1996. In contrast, U.S. exports of wheat to Canada have been less than 35 *tmt* per year, but were 62 *tmt* in the first ten months of 1996. Durum exports to the United States behave similarly, increasing from 370 *tmt* in 1990 to a high of 466 *tmt* in 1993, and declining to 182 *tmt* in 1995. Exports of Canadian barley to the United States follow a similar pattern, increasing from 389 *tmt* in 1990 to 1791 *tmt* in 1993, and then declining to 782 *tmt* in 1995. Although exports of malting barley were higher in

Figure 2: Canadian Barley Exports to the United States, by Type, 1990-96

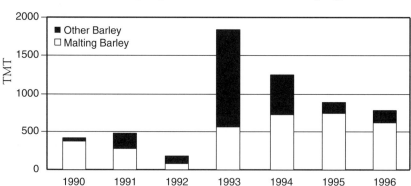

Figure 3: U.S. Wheat Exports to and Imports from Canada, 1990-96

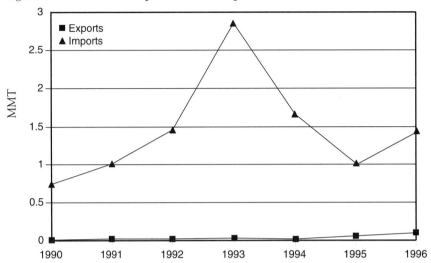

1993 than in 1990, most of the large volume of barley exports to the United States in 1993 was due to exports of feed barley.[3] U.S. exports of barley to Canada have been limited, but increased to 8.9 *tmt* in 1995. Canadian exports of oats have steadily increased from 171 *tmt* in 1990 to 1400 *tmt* in 1995, while U.S. exports of oats have been less than 3.1 *tmt*.

Wheat flour exports from Canada to the United States, similarly, have increased from 19 *tmt* in 1990 to 164 *tmt* in 1995 (Figure 6).[4]

Figure 4: U.S. Barley Exports to and Imports from Canada, 1990-96

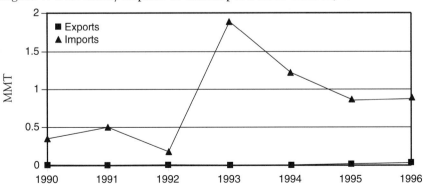

Figure 5: U.S. Oats Exports to and Imports from Canada, 1990-96

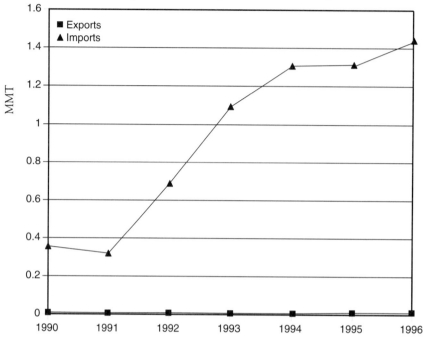

Much of this has been in spring wheat flour. Canadian exports of malt to the United States declined from 20 *tmt* in 1990 to 7.1 *tmt* in 1992. Since then, Canadian malt exports increased to 32 *tmt* in 1995. U.S. exports of malt to Canada were limited up to 1993, but increased to

Figure 6: U.S. Malt Exports to and Imports from Canada, 1990-95

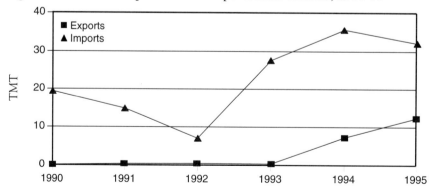

Figure 7: Canadian Exports and Imports of Gluten to the U.S., 1991-95

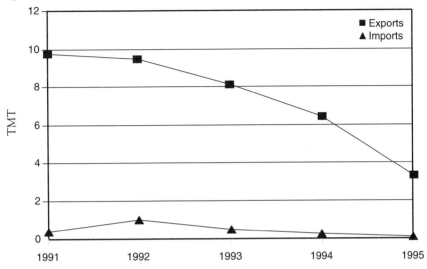

11.8 *tmt* in 1995 (Figure 7). Canadian exports of wheat gluten to the United States declined from 9,619 metric tonnes (*mt*) in 1991 to 3,176 *mt* in 1995. Imports of gluten from the United States have ranged from a high of 1,000 *mt* in 1992 to a low of 109 *mt* in 1995 (Figure 8). Canadian and U.S. export trade of starch for food use has fluctuated with

Figure 8: Canadian Exports and Imports of Starch–Food Use to the U.S., 1991-95

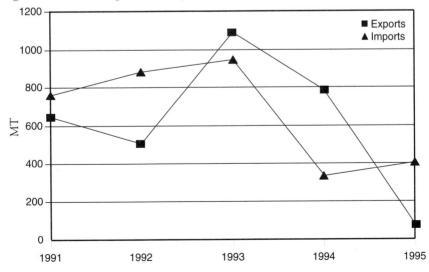

Figure 9: Canadian Exports and Imports of Starch–Industrial Use to the U.S., 1991-95

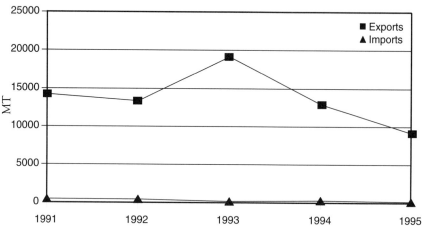

one country's exporting more than the other in different years. Canada has dominated export trade of starch for industrial use. U.S. exports of industrial-use starch have been less than 555 *mt*, while Canadian exports have ranged from a high of 19,234 *mt* in 1993 to a low of 9,255 *mt* in 1995 (Figure 9).

Trade Restrictions

Under the CUFTA, annual support levels for wheat, barley, and oats were measured for the United States and Canada to govern trade restrictions. Under the agreement, when U.S. support levels were less than Canadian support levels, Canadian import licenses would be removed. This occurred for oats in 1990 and wheat in 1991, and Canadian import licenses were removed for these commodities. However, primarily due to high Export Enhancement Program (EEP) subsidies for U.S. barley, import licenses remained for exports of barley to Canada.

The North American Free Trade Agreement (NAFTA) replaced the Canada-U.S. Free Trade Agreement (CUFTA) by incorporating the phase-out schedules contained in CUFTA. Additionally the NAFTA agreement assigned Canada increased global import quotas for chicken, turkey, and shell eggs, while the United States maintained the right to restrict imports to protect its price support programs for grains. Under Section 22, the United States applied Tariff Rate Quotas (TRQs) on wheat during September 1994-1995. These provisions resulted in a series of disputes and negotiations restricting imports of Canadian wheat, primarily durum (Gardner 1997). Under NAFTA, all tariffs (with few exceptions) were to be phased out by 1 January 1998.[5]

On 31 July 1995, Canada eliminated its import licensing requirements for wheat, barley, and their products on a Most-Favored Nation (MFN) basis. The next day, Canada implemented TRQs for these products. Under the WTO/Uruguay Round, nontariff barriers were converted to tariffs. Many import quotas were converted to TRQs, which provided for within-quota quantity and generally high over-quota tariffs. Under GATT requirements, TRQ access commitments are to be increased, within-quota tariff rates are subject to reduction, and over-quota tariff rates are to be lowered over six years.

In 1996, Canada applied the NAFTA tariff rates on wheat imported from the United States, but counted U.S. wheat imports toward WTO access commitments. For barley and malt, Canada did not apply the NAFTA tariff rates, but instead applied the higher WTO over-quota tariff rates. Canada argued that licensing requirements established before the WTO agreement allowed it to apply these over-quota tariff rates and TRQs and that this was consistent with NAFTA. The United States filed a complaint under NAFTA for these WTO tariffs for dairy, poultry, and barley products as applied to imports from the United States.

The United States lost this challenge. Canada won a unanimous decision by all panel members, indicating that Canada has the right to apply the tariffs that were agreed to in the WTO agreements on imports of U.S. dairy, poultry, egg, margarine, and barley products and that these tariffs are consistent with the provisions of NAFTA. Under NAFTA, Canada was allowed to maintain quantitative import restrictions against certain U.S. imports. However, under the WTO, Canada is obliged to end its quantitative import restrictions and has the right to convert them into tariff equivalents (Department of Foreign Affairs and International Trade 1996). The under-access tariff for barley and barley products was set to be eliminated in January 1998, and actual imports of barley have not reached the under-access limit. This suggests that other factors are limiting the movement of barley into Canada. Tariff rate quotas on barley and barley products were a major item at trade talks between U.S. and Canadian negotiators. Following these talks in Ottawa in September 1997, the

Canadian government indicated it would suspend application of tariff rate quotas on U.S. barley and barley products (Elliot 1997).

There were, as well, other restrictions to this trade. Under implementing legislation for NAFTA, the USDA was required to implement an end-use certificate system to monitor imports of all wheat or barley from all countries with similar requirements as of 8 April 1994. Canada was the only country imposing end-use certificates on U.S. wheat and, as such, is the only country affected by the regulations. End-use certificates were implemented on 27 February 1995 for all wheat entering the United States from Canada. Since Canada does not require end-use certificates on barley, end-use certificates were established for wheat only.

Final rules for end-use certificates require U.S. importers to store Canadian-produced wheat separately from other stocks to preserve its identity until it is delivered for export, or to the exporter, or end user. Importers can commingle Canadian and U.S. wheat when it is being loaded for delivery to the end user. However, exports of Canadian grain cannot be shipped under U.S. export subsidy and other export programs (including EEP, General Sales Manager [GSM], and PL480). End-use certificates were established to restrict the use of Canadian grain in U.S. export subsidy programs, but do not prohibit the commingling of Canadian wheat for use in domestic food aid programs. Importers are required to submit end-use certificates to the Farm Service Agency (FSA) within fifteen work days of the grain's entering the United States. All sales and resales of Canadian-produced wheat are required to be reported within fifteen days of the sale. Exporters and end users are also required to submit quarterly reports on consumption amounts and methods (USDA-ERS 1995; National Grain Trade Council 1995).

Canada also has import requirements for U.S. wheat. Imports for human consumption must have an end-use certificate and remain segregated from Canadian wheat.[6] Imports of U.S. wheat for feed must have a certain percentage that are colored and must be denatured. An import permit is required under the Plant Protection Act at no fee. In addition, a phytosanitary certificate must be obtained from the Canadian Grain Commission (CGC). Further, if delivery of U.S. wheat imports is to a licensed Canadian elevator, the elevator operator must have received prior authorization from the Canadian Grain Commission. CGC authorization will be given only if it is satisfied that elevator capacity and procedures would ensure that Canadian and U.S. grains would not be commingled (Agriculture Canada 1997). The Canadian government has indicated that these requirements are needed to maintain the integrity of the Canadian grain-handling system.

Debate has focused on removing end-use certificates in both Canada and the United States.[7] The Joint Commission on Grains proposed this change. The National Grain Trade Council indicated that end-use certificates will put increased demands on the domestic market and infrastructure. Significant reporting requirements are mandated, along with the requirement to preserve identity of the grain.

Beyond end-use certificates, Canada established restrictions for karnal bunt on imports of U.S. grains on 26 March 1996. Under this policy, durum wheat from the continental United States and barley, oats, sorghum, and millet from Arizona, California, New Mexico, and Texas are prohibited from entering Canada. Wheat other than durum, and other grains not infested with karnal bunt and flag smut and from an approved elevator on the U.S.-approved elevator list can enter Canada, but must be certified as karnal bunt-free (Alberta Agriculture 1996b). Proof of where the seed was grown must be provided. Also, imports of grain for seed into Canada are controlled by the Canada Seeds Act. Regulations to import grains for seed use are very extensive. Seed varieties must undergo a rigorous variety approval process to be sold in Canada. Varieties must meet requirements for agronomic, disease resistance, visual distinguishability, and end-use quality parameters. If varieties fail in any of these areas, they can be rejected. In the Canadian marketing system, varieties within a class must be visually distinguishable from other classes. Specifically, "the criteria for variety approval comprise scientific as well as non-scientific factors. This system of variety control is considered a key element of the Canadian grain quality system. The Canada Seeds Act regulations are currently under review; Agriculture Canada officials hope to finish a regulatory overhaul in Spring 1996" (USDA-FAS 1996, 43).[8] This requirement has been argued to reduce the number of varieties released and has been identified as one of the requirements that could potentially be changed.[9]

Factors Contributing to U.S. Imports

It is critical that the United States have policies that remove grain area from production. While there have been long-standing set-aside policies, which have been abandoned in recent years, a remaining program that has an important impact on supply is the Conservation Reserve

Program (CRP). Though, in aggregate, this policy has a potentially minor effect—though it has been criticized by the National Grain and Feed Association and others—it has a very important impact on some of the grains in question, notably durum wheat and barley. Under this program, significant acres were enrolled from 1986 to 1992. Wheat base acres entered were 411,000 from Minnesota; 1,051,763 from Montana; and 1,138,046 from North Dakota. Johnson and Wilson indicated that the CRP in barley has the effect of increasing Canadian barley prices and exports to the United States. A second factor to consider is that the United States is viewed as a large market, generally demanding higher quality grains and capable of paying premiums for these grains. To demonstrate the cumulative effect of both supply and demand on durum, as an example, Figure 10 shows U.S. supply and demand for higher grades of durum. As noted, since 1991 the U.S. has been a deficit producer, thus inducing imports.

In contrast, Canada has a relatively large excess supply of higher quality grains. It is important that the distribution of quality across grades of grain is comparable between the United States and Canada, as expected given that the weather-induced effects are similar. The fundamental difference is that Canada has a small domestic market, the cumulative effect being a larger excess supply of higher quality grains.[10] As examples, from 1985 to 1997, an average of 50 percent of Canadian Western Amber Durum (CWAD) production has been of grades CWAD 1 or CWAD 2, and an average of 23 percent of CWAD production has been consumed domestically in Canada. The distribution of grades is comparable in the United States, but a much larger percent is consumed domestically.

It is also important that there has been a drastic change in the composition of importers of Canadian grains in the past decade. Notable has been the reduction in shipments to Russia from Thunder Bay. Exports of wheat to the former Soviet Union dropped from 4,966 *tmt* in 1985-86 to 97 *tmt* in 1994-95 and durum exports, which had been increasing to a high of 1,294 *tmt* in 1991-92, were negligible in 1993-95. This is important because it has resulted in Canada's seeking new markets, which have been primarily importers from the western port areas, thereby causing capacity constraints in the west and surplus capacity in the east, which is the natural tributary to much of the U.S. market.

It is also important that there is a greater, and potentially growing frequency of, marketing capacity constraint in western Canada versus the

Figure 10: Production of No. 1 and No. 2 HAD and Domestic Consumption, U.S. by Year, 1980-97

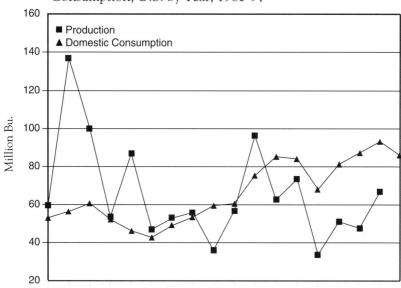

U.S. It is notable that: first, west-coast handlers are nearly always operating at capacity and, second, there are routine occurrences of rail car shortages, thereby requiring car allocation procedures. As a result, demurrage payments by the CWB have grown. This is important, because it has likely resulted in increased flows to the United States, which has the effect of relieving capacity elsewhere in the system.

Many of the previous studies and inquiries, and part of the political debate, have made the point that one reason for Canadian exports to the United States during that period was the EEP. Simply, when export price subsidies are used, it depresses the offshore market and increases the U.S. domestic market. The combination of these produced immense price differentials between the markets and, thus, incentives and pressures for Canada to export to the United States. Johnson and Wilson demonstrate the impact of EEP on trade flows in the North American market. Most important is that EEP had the effect of increasing Canadian prices by 7¢/bushel and flows from Canada to the United States by 870,000 *mt*. Interestingly, that program had not been used since July 1995, but exports to the United

States approached record levels in 1996-97 (a year of concurrent crop deficits in the U.S. and a catastrophic transport situation in Canada), thus suggesting that there is more at play than simply the EEP—which incidently was supported by Johnson and Wilson.

In addition, lower rail rates on grain to export (offshore) position had the effect of subsidizing exports and thereby favoring those movements. These were eliminated in 1996, making marginal sales into and/ or through the U.S. relatively more attractive.

One of the effects of price pooling in Canada is to create relatively constant prices (that is, the local price of the initial payment) to farmers within the market year. In contrast, spot prices in the U.S. vary continuously. Thus, in a bullish market, and/or if CWB initial payments are depressed, there are incentives to try to bypass the Canadian market and ship to the U.S.

And even though some trade barriers remain, there are commercial and competitive pressures for these market systems to become more integrated. This is a natural evolution and results from the combined effects of comparative advantage, competition, and firm strategies. In addition, globalization of many industries results in pressure for greater integration. Industrial integration will likely be a two-stage process. First, the industries will become more integrated—while retaining conventional business practices. This is the thrust of many of the current changes. The second stage will be an integration of business practices—or convergence of business practices. This is exactly what is being observed in North American grain-handling, shipping, and processing sectors. These changes, along with remaining differences, are described in the section to follow.

The U.S. grain-handling system has been evolving for some time, whereas Canada's has been accelerated substantially, due to a multitude of microeconomic pressures induced by the integration of the two countries' grain-marketing economies. During the past decade, there have been radical changes in the structure of the Canadian grain-marketing system. While the dynamics of these changes seem extreme, it is important to realize that they are likely a result of the cumulative impacts of numerous pressures.

Before the early 1990s, the Canadian grain-handling industry was largely dominated by Canadian pools and a few Canadian private firms. The only major U.S. firm with Canadian handling assets was Cargill, which had been in Canada for many years. Numerous pressures have emerged for structural changes including, but not limited to, changes in the rail rate regime and the emergence of a North American marketplace for procurement.

As a result of these and the ensuing competitive dynamics, there have been numerous changes. Each of the Canadian firms and pools is in the process of rationalizing its own systems, resulting in fewer larger-scale country elevators. It is notable that, in many cases, these new facilities have the ability to condition grains at the origin, in a manner similar to that traditionally being employed exclusively at export terminals. In addition, two major U.S. firms have entered the industry. ConAgra has entered with new construction of country elevators throughout the prairies, and Archer Daniels Midland (ADM) created a strategic alliance with United Grain Growers (UGG) with options for procurement. Potential reasons for these changes include: procurement strategy for northern-tier small grains; inability to create strategic ventures with incumbents for supply agreements; dynamics of structural change favors entrants; they are Canadian rail-induced; they are a longer-term strategy to rival northern-tier U.S. railroads. The cumulative effect of these changes will likely create an environment with excess handling capacity, greater efficiency, lower marginal costs, and more intense competition for origination.

There have also been changes that may or will directly make crossborder shipping more efficient and attractive. One of these has been the establishment of handling facilities located at U.S. border points with rail access. These include the joint ventures between Alberta Pool and General Mills at Sweetgrass, Montana, and the venture between Saskatchewan Wheat Pool and General Mills at Northgate, North Dakota. While some have initially promoted these as being primarily for shipment from Canada to the United States, their strategic development has been to encourage and facilitate trade in both directions, varying by commodity and depending on market conditions over time. These are likely natural logistical channels for shipping U.S. feed grains into western Canada and potentially for shipping U.S. grains through Canada to offshore export.

A related change that has potential long-term implications is an announced expansion of export-handling capacity at Roberts Bank in southern British Columbia. This is notable because west coast handling capacity in southern Canada has been constrained which, in fact, is likely an important cause for the escalation of movements of Canadian grain to and through the United States. This constraint has also generally limited the ability of U.S. grains moving to and through Canada. In the future, this expansion could provide the capacity relief necessary to expand Canadian west-coast exports.

In addition to these changes, there have been notable structural changes in the Canadian grain-processing sector. First, due to growth in the Alberta feeding industry, that province has gone from being a large feed surplus region to potentially and periodically a feed deficit region.[11] In addition, ConAgra has announced a proposed biofuel additive plant to be located in Alberta.

The second important change is that several of the major grain-processing firms have been acquired by U.S. firms. One of the most intriguing areas is malting where, prior to 1990, Canadian firms were 100 percent Canadian. Since then, a joint venture was formed between Schreier (U.S.) and Prairie Malt, which was recently sold to Cargill; Rahr (U.S.) has entered Canada with a plant in Alix, Alberta; and Canada Malt, the largest malting company in Canada, was acquired by ConAgra.[12]

A similar transition occurred in flour milling. Before 1990, all Canadian plants were Canadian-owned except Robin Hood (International Multifoods), and bakers were highly vertically integrated into milling—in contrast to the U.S. Anticipating the potential competitive effects of the CUFTA, the two major Canadian flour-milling companies sought to merge in order to be competitive in U.S.-Canada trade, but were rejected due to antitrust concerns. Nearly immediately, these firms were sold, respectively, to ADM and ConAgra, two of the three largest milling firms in the U.S. Since then, ConAgra and ADM dominated and the ConAgra/MapleLeaf joint venture was acquired by ADM. Thus, 70 percent of Canadian capacity is owned by one U.S. firm—ADM. ADM (through acquisitions of Canadian-owned plants and, subsequently, a major acquisition of plants owned by a joint venture between MapleLeaf Foods and ConAgra) has established the domineering position (Wilson 1995). Similar transitions are occurring in oilseed processing (Johnson 1995) and the meat sector. In general, a convergence of players is occurring in major grain-processing industries. Virtually all of the major processing sectors in Canada have become dominated by U.S.-based firms since the late 1980s. Finally, it is interesting to note that, in the railroad industry, the Canadian Pacific acquired the SooLine, a major northern-tier U.S. railroad. The Canadian National was privatized, but has entered into joint line agreements to gain access to the U.S. market, and has recently sought acquisitions in the U.S.

Marketing System Differences and Changes toward Integration

Future crossborder trade prospects will be affected in part by the trade policy environment, but also by differences and commercial changes in the marketing system. There are several important differences between these marketing systems. In addition, some important changes are occurring.

Important differences between the rail shipping systems in the two countries could have a very important effect on future trade flows. One is that, though Canadian rail rates have been increased, they are still lower than those that apply from similar U.S. shipping points. These differences are particularly notable in the northern-tier regions of North Dakota and Montana.[13] If everything else is the same with equal access, this difference is important because it should induce some U.S. grain to move to or through the Canadian marketing system. Through this process, the potential for crossborder trade would provide competition to shipping regimes for U.S. grains. In contrast, Canadian shippers are not treated differently when using the U.S. transportation system and generally have equal access to its capacity at nondiscriminatory rates. This would not be true for U.S. shipments through Canada.

Railcar allocation in Canada is highly controlled based on past shipping practices. One important distinction is between the allocation of cars for shipment of CWB grains versus nonboard commodities. CWB cars are allocated by the railroads for movements of CWB grains, and those cars are allocated by the CWB to its designated shippers and train runs (zones have been proposed) for the movements of CWB grains.[14] The other portion is allocated by the CAPG (Car Allocation Policy Group, a temporary mechanism to replace a previous regime called the Grain Transportation Authority) as nonboard allocator, for the movement of nonboard grains (that is, for movements not controlled by the CWB). Normally, these are oats, canola, and others, but would also include any shipments of U.S. grains to or through the Canadian grain-marketing system. Thus, allocation of railcars in Canada for shipment of U.S. grains could affect the viability of trade flows to the extent that there are differences between CWB and non-CWB grains. This is in contrast to U.S. railroads, which do not distinguish country of origin in allocation of cars; that is, Canadian shippers have equal access to U.S. railcars through tariff and contractual allocation mechanisms.

The regulation of rail rates on grain is also important. Changes in the Western Grain Transportation Act (WGTA) increased rail shipping costs paid directly by shippers (previously, the total cost was comparable, but a portion was paid directly by the government of Canada to the railroads). It is important that the new higher rail rates (specifically, that portion paid by the shipper) are still substantially less than comparable rates in the United States. However, the legislation states specifically that these rates are for the movements of "any grain or crop included in Schedule II that is grown in the Western Division... for movements to Thunder Bay or Armstrong... and specifically excludes shipment to British Columbia ports for shipment to the United States" (Canada Transportation Act, Division VI *Transportation of Western Grain*, 70). Thus, any U.S. grain moving to or through Canada would not necessarily have access to these rates.

The underlying legislation provides the formula for rate determination and describes its application. Specifically, it establishes a maximum rate scale. These rates are frozen to the year 1999, at which time they become subject to the CTA, unless challenged otherwise.[15] The important point is that this is a much different regulatory regime than exists in the United States, and it clearly applies only to grains grown in western Canada.

Reciprocal Access: Principal Issues

The Joint Commission also indicated that a longer-term objective is to provide reciprocal access over time (95). Issues surrounding the idea of reciprocal access were identified in a number of the research papers prepared for the commission. Though the concept was not completely defined, several authors discussed it. One of the visions of the Joint Commission was that, ultimately, pressures will escalate for greater integration between the marketing systems in Canada and the United States. The commercial process toward integration of these systems has escalated, which, in the future, will add to pressures to harmonize as much as possible marketing, and possibly policy, mechanisms.

For these reasons, the term reciprocal access has been promoted as a concept for discussion about changes to reduce trade frictions. This term was conceived during the Joint Commission process and ultimately held as an ideal longer-term goal.[16] Reciprocal access is an acknowledgment that each country's marketing and policy mechanisms have certain positive virtues and, in a more integrated environment, should be accessible to growers on each side of the border.

Notwithstanding the trade barriers, reciprocal access should be viewed as a longer-term goal. The concept can be addressed in two ways. One is from the perspective of broader policy mechanisms, in which growers would have reciprocal access. The other is that growers would have reciprocal access to certain features of each country's marketing mechanisms and infrastructure.

Farm policy mechanisms on each side of the border have effects on either price differentials and/or trade flows. Of particular importance and interest in the United States are the EEP (supporting U.S. prices relative to Canadian and offshore) and CRP (resulting in reduced production in the United States and, therefore, supporting prices). In Canada, these would include the initial payment guarantees and the pooling system. However, given the sovereignty of each of these countries and their programs, reciprocal access at this broad level is not likely achievable.

In a marketplace with greater reciprocal access, crossborder trade may occur due to differences in marketing costs. However, some important competitive functions of the marketing system in each country are denied crossborder participants in some cases. In Canada, these include CWB marketing mechanisms to capture premiums,[17] lower rail rates, and preferred car allocations. These marketing functions are limited to operate solely for grains produced in western Canada. In contrast, when and as Canadian grain is exported to or through the United States, it has full nondiscriminatory access to comparable U.S. functions. The U.S. handling and shipping system generally has adequate capacity and is efficient enough to induce crossborder shipments. These are purely commercial and nondiscriminatory with respect to country of origin.

Reciprocal access involves having access to each country's marketing system (and policy infrastructure). Potential benefits of the U.S. marketing system include access to transport infrastructure (rail, road infrastructure, barges, and port infrastructure), elevators, and risk transfer through U.S. futures markets. While these are primarily a result of commercial relationships and mechanisms, in a number of dimensions, the public sector is involved through providing infrastructure, services, and a regulatory framework. There is minimal movement of U.S. grains to or through Canada; however, in the future (with expansion of west-coast ports and more direct crossborder and bilateral linkages), the likelihood and frequency of U.S. grains moving to or through Canadian infrastructure will increase. At that time, issues related to these barriers and differences will escalate.

Conclusion: Pressures for Change

Numerous pressures have evolved to integrate the grain-marketing systems in North America. Most important among these are differences in relative supply and demand for specific grain qualities, and the demand for alternative logistical channels given changes in world grain trade. In addition, differences in farm and export policy mechanisms have, in some cases, induced trade distortions and hampered an easy transition to a more fully harmonized system.

Commercially, the grains sector of North America is becoming harmonized more rapidly than is the policy environment. The commercial integration will likely be a two-stage process. First, firms will become more integrated through asset ownership. As this is being done, the next stage will be pressures to standardize commercial practices across the geographic region. This is the stage that is yet to evolve. It is interesting that the commercial integration is leading the way, though it would likely be preferable if the policy environment were harmonized first. The fact that the commercial sector is leading the move toward integration suggests that eventually it will provide added pressure to harmonize the policy differences.

As these systems become more integrated there are lessons for each country. For the United States it is important to recognize that farm and export policy mechanisms that are initiated unilaterally are antiquated, largely ineffective, and counterproductive within a freer North American marketing system. Notable among these are the CRP and EEP programs, both of which were conceived in an era prior to freer trade within North America. In addition, commercially, it is important to note that a portion of the trade that has been induced has been in response to quality shortages and, particularly, the effects of vomitoxin in the northern plains.

A number of issues continue to be important to Canada and will evolve as these systems integrate. The CWB will continue to be the focal point, both within Canada and from the United States. Pressure from the latter will persist so long as the CWB is perceived to have some instilled advantages due to its statutory nature, relative to non-statutory rivals. In addition to this pressure which is not new, two others will likely become important. One is that pressure will eventually emerge on the transaction costs associated with CWB marketings. New entrants into the Canadian grain-marketing system were induced partly due to the opportunities associated with rapid structural changes in the industry, and to rival the potential market power of incumbents. However, no doubt, once the initial structural dynamics are determined, one of the objectives that will emerge from these new rivals will be to exploit vertical efficiencies, in part due to intrafirm transactions. In the process, if intrafirm transaction costs are less than those of conventional procurement practices, then purchasing through the CWB system will be challenged.

The second pressure will emerge in response to the apparent discriminatory nature of some of the policies governing grain marketing in Canada, which gives domestically produced grains an advantage in movements through Canada relative to those produced in the United States. Reciprocal access is already an important issue confronting the future North American grain-marketing system. Recognizing that each country's marketing and policy mechanisms have certain positive virtues is important, and the major issue is the extent that these should be accessible to growers on each side of the border. There are important differences in the marketing mechanisms (functions) and commercial environments that determine their bilateral accessibility. In general, in the United States, these functions are performed nondiscriminatorily with respect to country of origin. In contrast, in Canada, there are several very important functions (notably those related to shipping and handling) that would treat U.S. grains differently from Canadian grains.

NOTES

1. This paper draws liberally from a longer paper by Wilson and Dahl, 1998.

2. See Wilson and Dahl for a summary of these studies.

3. This is likely due to important differences in malting barley varieties (Wilson and Johnson 1995a) which may have constrained the potential for increased flows from Canada to the United States.

4. In addition to these grains and semiprocessed products, the volume of trade in further processed and consumer products has escalated. See Krause, Dooley, and Wilson for a summary of that trade.

5. NAFTA tariff rates for market access to Canada for specified commodities in 1996.

6. However, these end-use certificates destroy the opportunity for resale of the grain, thus reducing the flexibility of Canadian end-users.

7. This debate continues. U.S.-Canada discussions in Ottawa focused on end-use certificates with further talks scheduled (Elliot).

8. This was completed in Spring 1997.

9. Dahl and Wilson provide an extensive review of these provisions and differences.

10. Dahl and Wilson provide detailed quantitative estimates of these values.

11. An important movement is for barley to be shipped from Saskatchewan to Alberta, and periodically other feeds are shipped from the United States.

12. Wilson and Johnson (1995b) provide a description of the globalization of the malt industry, and Wilson describes similar changes in flour.

13. Fulton and Gray indicated that these differences are as much as $1/bushel.

14. This system is under dispute in Canada and is under pressure for change. For an extensive review of the evolution of car allocation in the United States, see Priewe and Wilson. This is notwithstanding the potential implications of various forms of government-owned cars in Canada.

15. This is likely one of the goals of the CTA dispute about Canadian grain shipments.

16. In trade discussions reported in January 1998, the United States suggested a pilot project to allow U.S. grain to be shipped directly to Canadian elevators. This is obviously an effort toward effectuating the possibility of reciprocal trade (*Western Producer*).

17. Kraft et al. demonstrate that the CWB is capable of capturing premiums relative to a system with multiple sellers.

REFERENCES

Abel, Martin E. 1995. *A Comparison of the U.S. and Canadian Marketing Systems for Wheat and Barley: Transparency, Differential Pricing, and Monopolistic Behavior.* Paper prepared for the Canada/U.S. Joint Commission on Grains, New Orleans, 22-23 February.

Agriculture Canada. 1997. *How to Export Wheat and Barley to Canada: Fact Sheets.* August.

Alberta Agriculture. 1996a. *Canada-U.S. Trade.* Alberta Agriculture, Food and Rural Development's Policy Secretariat and Market Analysis and Statistics Branch. Edmonton, 19 November, 2.

_____. 1996b. "Canada's Interim Policy on Imports of U.S. Grains." *Canada-U.S. Trade.* Alberta Agriculture, Food and Rural Development's Policy Secretariat and Market Analysis and Statistics Branch. Edmonton, 12 May, 1.

Alston, J.M., R. Gray, and D.A. Sumner. 1994. "The Wheat War of 1994." *Canadian Journal of Agricultural Economics* 42: 231-51.

Canada Grains Council. 1996. *Canadian Grains Industry Statistical Handbook 96.* Winnipeg: Canada Grains Council.

Canada-United States Joint Commission on Grains. 1995. *Canada-United States Joint Commission on Grains Final Report.* Washington. October.

Dahl, Bruce L., and William W. Wilson. 1997. *Factors Affecting the Supply of High Quality Spring Wheats: Comparisons Between the United States and Canada.* Agricultural Economics Report No. 374, Department of Agricultural Economics. Fargo: North Dakota State University, May.

Department of Foreign Affairs and International Trade. 1996. *Ministers Welcome NAFTA Panel Decision.* Department of Foreign Affairs and International Trade-Canada, No. 229. Ottawa, 2 December. http://www.dfait-maeci.gc.ca/english/news/press_~1/96_press/96_229E.HTM

Elliot, Ian. 1997. "U.S. Negotiators Continue Talks with Canada Over Grain." *Feedstuffs* (22 September): 15.

Fulton, Murray, and Richard Gray. 1997. *Railways, Competition and the Hold-Up Problem.* Paper presented at Agricultural Research Symposium titled "The Economics of World Wheat Markets: Implications for the Northern Rockies and Great Plains." Trade Research Center, Montana State University, Bozeman, 1 June.

Furtan, W.H. 1995. *Transparency and Differential Pricing: An Analysis of Canadian and American Grain Handling Systems.* Paper prepared for the Canada/U.S. Joint Commission on Grains, New Orleans, 22-23 February.

Gardner, Bruce L. 1997. *Canada/U.S. Farm Policies and the Creation of a Single North American Grain Market.* Paper presented at the Economics of World Wheat Markets Research Symposium sponsored by the Trade Research Center, Montana State University, Bozeman, 29 May – 2 June.

Gray, Richard, and Bruce Gardner. 1995. *The Impact of Canadian and U.S. Farm Policies on Grain Production and Trade.* Paper prepared for the Canada/U.S. Joint Commission on Grains, New Orleans, 22-23 February.

Johnson, D., and W. Wilson. 1995. "Canadian Rail Subsidies and Continental Barley Flows: A Spatial Analysis." *Logistics and Transportation Review* 31: 31-46.7e.

Kraft, D., H. Furtan, and E. Tyrchniewicz. 1996. *Performance Evaluation of the Canadian Wheat Board.* Winnipeg.

Krause, Joyce H., Frank J. Dooley, and William W. Wilson. 1995. *Global Import Demand for Value-Added Wheat Products*. Agricultural Economics Report No. 325. Department of Agricultural Economics, North Dakota State University, Fargo, January.

Loyns, R.M.A., and Maurice Kraut. 1995. *Pricing to Value in the Canadian Grain Industry*. Paper prepared for the Canada/U.S. Joint Commission on Grains, New Orleans, 22-23 February.

Marsh, J., and J. Johnson. 1995. "Changes in Wheat Stocks and Cash Price." *Montana Agricultural Research* 12(Spring): 19-22.

National Grain Trade Council. 1995. *Issue Update: USDA Issues Final End-Use Certificate Rules*. Report presented by the National Grain Trade Council, La Jolla, CA, 10-11 February, 19-20.

Priewe, Steven R., and William W. Wilson. 1997. *Forward Shipping Options for Grain by Rail: A Strategic Analysis*. Agricultural Economics Report No. 372, Department of Agricultural Economics, North Dakota State University, Fargo.

Producer Payment Panel. 1994. *Delivering the Western Grain Transportation Act Benefit to Producers: Technical Appendix*. Winnipeg, June.

Transport Institute. 1996. *Future Changes in Eastbound Grain Traffic*. The International Institute for Sustainable Development, The University of Manitoba, Winnipeg, 77.

United States Department of Agriculture-Economic Research Service (USDA-ERS). 1995. *Wheat Situation Yearbook*. Washington: USDA-ERS, February.

United States Department of Agriculture-Foreign Agriculture Service (USDA-FAS). 1996. *Grain and Feed Annual Attache Report-Canada*. Washington: USDA-FAS, 26 March, 57.

Western Grain Marketing Panel. 1996. *Grain Marketing*. Winnipeg: Western Grain Marketing Panel, 1 July.

Western Producer. 1998. "Ag Leaders Discuss CWB Audit, Freer Grain Trade," *Western Producer* (22 January): 12.

Wilson, William W. 1995. "Structural Changes and Strategies in the North American Flour Milling Industry." *Agribusiness: An International Journal* 11: 431- 40.

Wilson, W., and D. Johnson. 1995a. "North American Malting Barley Trade: Impacts of Differences in Quality and Marketing Costs." *Canadian Journal of Agricultural Economics* 43: 335-53.

_____. 1995b. "Competition and Policy Conflicts in Canada-U.S. Barley Trade." *Journal of Agriculture and Resource Economics* 20: 64-81.

Wilson, W., D. Johnson, and B. Dahl. 1995. *Pricing to Value*. Paper prepared for the Canada/U.S. Joint Commission on Grains, New Orleans, 22-23 February.

Wilson, W., and Bruce L. Dahl. 1998. *Reciprocal Access in U.S./Canadian Grain Trade: Background Issues for the U.S. Grain Trade*. Department of Agricultural Economics, Report No. AE 98001, January.

Young, Linda M. 1996. *Changing Canadian Grain Policies: Implications for Montana's Grain Industry*. Policy Issues Paper No. 1. Bozeman: Northern Plains and Rockies Center for the Study of Western Hemisphere Trade, 31.

Contributors

VINCENT AMANOR-BOADU is Associate Director at the George Morris Centre, University of Guelph. He has published and presented numerous papers and reports dealing with Canada's agrifood competitiveness, trade agreements, biotechnology policy, and strategic alliances. He is an editorial advisor of *Supply Chain Management*.

MEL ANNAND practices law in Melfort, Saskatchewan. He has lectured in the areas of Economics, Business Law, Law Office Administration, and Agricultural Law. Annand completed a Master of Laws degree in International Trade at the University of Saskatchewan in 1998. He has served as a Bencher in the Law Society and was a founding Board member and Vice Chairman (1992-1995) of the Saskatchewan Legal Education Society. He was designated Queen's counsel in 1994.

KATHERINE BAYLIS is a Research Assistant in the Département d'Économie Agro-alimentaire at Université Laval. She recently completed her M.Sc. in Agricultural Economics at the University of Saskatchewan. Prior to returning to do her graduate work, she was Executive Secretary of the National Farmers Union in Canada. She is currently working on a textbook on Canadian agricultural policy.

BRUCE L. DAHL is Research Scientist in the Department of Agricultural Economics at North Dakota State University.

HARTLEY FURTAN is Professor of Agricultural Economics, University of Saskatchewan. His area of teaching and research is Canadian agricultural policy. He was Deputy Minister of Agriculture and Food, Province of Saskatchewan, from 1993 to 1995.

RICHARD S. GRAY is Associate Professor, Department of Agricultural Economics, and Director of the Centre for Studies in Agriculture Law and Environment at the University of Saskatchewan. He has written or coauthored numerous books, articles, papers, and reports, has lectured extensively, and has served as Crop Market Analyst with the Saskatchewan Department of Agriculture.

DEMCEY JOHNSON is Associate Professor in the Department of Agricultural Economics at North Dakota State University. His research focuses on marketing, trade, and agricultural price analysis.

GREGORY P. MARCHILDON is currently Deputy Minister to the Premier and Cabinet Secretary for the Saskatchewan government as well as an Adjunct Professor in the Faculty of Administration, University of Regina. After receiving his Ph.D. in economic history from the London School of Economics and Political Science, he taught for five years at Johns Hopkins University's School of Advanced International Studies. He has written numerous journal articles and is the author of *Profits and Politics: Beaverbrook and the Gilded Age of Canadian Finance* (1996).

JOHN M. MARSH is a Professor of Agricultural Economics and Economics at Montana State University-Bozeman. He has published in the areas of livestock and meat demand and supply and marketing issues. He also conducts research in livestock and meat trade issues relevant to NAFTA and GATT .

LARRY J. MARTIN is Chief Executive Officer at the George Morris Centre, University of Guelph. He has published and presented numerous papers and reports dealing with Canada's agrifood competitiveness, trade agreements, and trade disputes and served as expert witness in several Canada-U.S. trade disputes.

FIONA STIRLING is a Research Assistant at the George Morris Centre, University of Guelph. She recently completed her B. Comm. in Agricultural Business at the University of Guelph and is currently working on her M.B.A. at York University.

WILLIAM W. WILSON is Professor of Agricultural Economics at North Dakota State University. His areas of concentration include agribusiness, commodity marketing, and Canada-U.S. trade relationships. He is on the Board of Directors of the Minneapolis Grain Exchange and has served as a consultant to numerous agribusinesses throughout the world.

LINDA M. YOUNG is the Agricultural Policy Coordinator, Trade Research Center, Montana State University-Bozeman. She obtained her Ph.D. from the University of California-Davis. Her research interests include agricultural policy and trade, emphasizing the grain and livestock markets.

Index